*The earth has no edges these days;
the countries of the old Inca empire
are not that far away.
Yet Ecuador, Peru and Bolivia
still seem just a bit remote
from a world of instant travel
and communication.*

HIGH CITIES

OF THE

ANDES

Country band—Ecuador

WIDE WORLD PUBLISHING/TETRA

front cover photograph: near Cuzco by Marion Rust
back cover photograph: Machu Picchu by Gerald Charm
interior photos by Celia Wakefield unless otherwise indicated

Wide World Publishing/Tetra
P.O. Box 476
San Carlos, CA 94070

1st printing 1988
Printed in the United States of America.

Library of Congress Cataloging-in-Publication Data

Wakefield, Ceiia, 1916–.
    High Cities of the Andes.

    Biobliography: p.
    Includes index.
    1.Andes Region—Description and travel—1981–
2. Cities and towns—Andes Region.   3. Cities and towns,
Ruined, extinct, etc.—Andes Region.   4. Andes Region—
Social life and customs. 5. Andes Region— History,
Local.   6. Wakefield, Celia, 1916–   —Journeys—Andes
Region.   I. Title.
F2212.W35 1988   980   88-50273
ISBN 0-933174-58-6

CONTENTS

INTRODUCTION 1

I. PERU 5
The Navel of the World

II. BOLIVIA 45
Fresh Fried Truth

III. BOLIVIA 75
A City of Blood and Silver

IV. PERU 103
A Group of One

V. ECUADOR 115
The Two Faces of Quito

VI. ECUADOR 125
Cinnamon and Gold

VII. ECUADOR 133
The Athens of Ecuador

VIII. ECUADOR 147
How Round is the World?

IX. ECUADOR 155
Darkness at Noon

X. EPILOGUE 169

Bibliography

Index

Llamas roam among the high lagoons of Cajas.

Introduction

CAMÍNA EL AVTOR

The author and her travels

All my life I have felt a periodic urge to move on. This has led me to New York, Paris, Morocco. It has led me to crew on a sailboat from Hawaii to Alaska, to move to Mexico City on a one-way ticket. I have come to recognize the first stirring of restlessness as a hummingbird or butterfly recognizes the season to migrate. Why this happens I have never known. Many people seem to reside comfortably in one place for years, even to get homesick when they leave it.

Perhaps I am trying to escape, from myself, from other people, from responsibilities. That might be a reason for leaving, but not for arriving, with a light heart and perpetually eager expectations, at a new experience in life.

Travel has not been a career for me. It has been interrupted often and for long periods by mundane static jobs. Those desk-bound years run together in my memory, unimportant, marking time. What I remember with delight, after more than seven decades of living, are the periods of freedom, of travel.

Now in this book, at last, I will try to record the pleasures, pains and subtle impressions which an alien culture has given me. The earth has no edges these days; the countries of the old Inca empire are not that far away. Yet Ecuador, Peru and Bolivia still seem just a bit remote from a world of instant travel and communication.

On my first trip to South America three years ago, I was immediately captivated by the friendliness of the people of Peru, the grandeur of the landscape, and the awe-inspiring relics of ancient civilizations. When I planned to return for the third time last year, a friend remarked, "Why do you keep going down there? There's nothing to see but a few old Inca ruins." There's a world to be seen, and what is not visible of the past hangs invisibly in the air.

The high country of western South America has been occupied for thousands of years. We know little of the pre-Inca civilizations, but the Incas subdued almost a hundred tribes, indoctrinating them into their own civilization. The Inca empire, at its height, extended from what is now Columbia in the north to Chile in the south, its central area comprising Ecuador, Peru and Bolivia, an enormous territory which the Incas kept under control with iron supervision. Their civilization lasted only a little over 300 years from its beginning, was at its height for less than a century before the Spanish conquered it in 1535. Today, only the huge physical foundations of empire remain, in ruins, but there are still several million people speaking the Inca language, Quechua, and others around Lake Titicaca who speak the old Aymara tongue. The civilization and religion of these peoples were ruthlessly destroyed by the Spaniards in favor of the "True European Way", but much still remains of folklore and customs, from the adding of a stone to an Apachita at the top of a hill by passing travelers, to the divining of fortunes through the fetuses of llamas in La Paz' Street of Witches. A foreigner cannot hope to do more than scratch the surface of this many-layered civilization, but even a glimpse here and there adds to the interest of a visit to South America's cities of the high Andes.

Market vendors and the church against a cloudy sky—Peru

Cuzco— photo by Gerald Charm

PERU
The Navel of the World

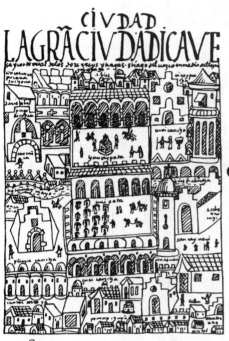

Cuzco

•*Cuzco*
•*Machu Picchu*

Everything in the Inca world was alive, sentient, the universe and all its contents sacred. There was no such thing as a dead object, whether stone, rainbow or river.

***

If anyone has ever entered Machu Picchu without amazement and awe, I have never heard of such a person. The fact that almost everyone has seen pictures and read descriptions makes no difference to the supreme moment. Not only are the ruins a magnificent, long-gone city, a place of memories, but the Incas built their aerie in a great location, as though envisaging the thousands of visitors who would, at this late date, visit their city.

Pedro de Cieza de Leon, first European to record impressions of the Andean country of Peru, left Spain at age thirteen on the ship *Cifuente* from Seville to Cartagena. In the sixteenth century such sea voyages were rugged. They took about forty days for the Atlantic crossing. No arrangements were made for passengers, who camped on deck with their own bedding and provisions. Thin mattresses were stuffed with dog hair and goatskin blankets provided some warmth. A passenger might eat "a morsel of bacon in the morning, a bit of cooked dried beef and some cheese at mid-day, and the same for supper."

Peruvian textile design

Cieza de Leon was no doubt a sturdy thirteen-year-old. He survived the voyage and spent seventeen years in the Americas. At the age of twenty he began his journal because "there came over me a great desire to relate the admirable things that have existed and much of what I have written I have seen with my own eyes." He described the invading Spaniards and the defeated Incas giving, as he put it, the "whole history of two separate races of men." He used a condor's quill for a pen, the top of a drumhead for a desk.

I thought of Cieza de Leon as I waited in Mexico City for the night flight to Lima. The wait was long. Our plane was coming from Los Angeles, where the crew must have gone to a late movie. Eventually it arrived and there was a mad rush to get on, men, women and children bouncing off each other in the narrow doorway while the ticket man yelled, "One line, just *one* line!" There were enough places, but just enough, and we had no assigned seats so the strife continued. The aisle was crammed with children perched on suitcases, with hatboxes disgorging clothes, with giant Mexican charro hats, souvenirs which took up as much space as though they had Mexicans beneath them.

An attendant tried to weed things out. Ahead of me a woman struggled with a bulky suitcase, a guitar and a baby.

"Carry-on baggage, Señora?" The attendant spoke severely. "You are taking aboard a great deal of luggage."

The woman reached back to haul up an outsized duffle bag. "Yes, I am." She disappeared with her trophies into the maw of the aircraft.

In my travels I have brought to near perfection the art of traveling light. Why check things on a plane when they may arrive in London instead of Lima. On this trip I took two 35 millimeter cameras (one for color, one for black-and-white), film, toilet articles, all in my camera bag, and in a canvas carry-on sack a couple of changes of clothes, extra shoes, and a notebook to record my impressions. I followed the lead of Spanish conquistadors who journeyed for months at a time with only their guns, shields, and small bags of belongings.

During that night flight from Mexico to Lima, the stars in the sky were much nearer than an Inca emperor could have imagined. He would, supposing he was aboard, demand more comforts than the airline was inclined to offer. He would, of course, occupy first class with his retinue, while we the "worthless people" crowded together in economy. He would be wearing all the signs of Inca royalty: the narrow head band with three small feathers and a silver disk, the embroidered tunic of fine wool, earplugs the size of oranges in the stretched lobes of his ears, showing him to be *cori rincri*, one of the men with "golden ears." Most important, he would wear the imperial scarlet fringe hanging over his eyes and nose. His reclining seat would be of gold with a vicuña fur head rest, and he would hold in his hand a glass of the universal drink of his days, the corn liquor *chicha*, while two gorgeous female flight attendants prostrated themselves in fear and veneration before his shining golden sandals.

Looking out the plane window the Inca would see a familiar sight: the

Southern Cross, a group of stars known to be a celestial llama with her young, browsing the heavenly *puna*. Perhaps he might glimpse the moon, half full now, and know it to be the source of silver through its tears, just as gold comes from the sweat of the sun. Yet even the Inca, supreme ruler on earth, would surely be astounded by the speed and efficiency with which an enormous metal monster hurtled through the star-spangled night.

Beside me, in the economy section where we were trying to get comfortable, a Bolivian mother quieted her child, who refused to sleep, with riddles. The Spanish brought riddles to the high country, and both Aymara and Quechua people took them up.

"Who caresses your face, but you can never see her?" The child shook her head as the mother passed her hand along her cheek. "The wind, of course, the wind. Try another one, Chica."

I recognized this one: "What is the banknote that cannot be folded, and the change which cannot be counted?"

The child muttered drowsily, "The sky and the stars."

I was glad she knew the answer — she had probably heard the riddle a hundred times. The punishment for not knowing the answer is supposed to be "El Rinki," eating a dead burro. Of course you can avoid this by kissing an old witch's butt and she will give you the answer. The child made no further complaint, and fell asleep.

As we swooped low over Callao at the Pacific's edge, preparing for our landing in Lima, the Sapa Inca, the Royal Emperor, would see his ancestor, Inti, the Sun, rising over the land. He would push back the scarlet imperial fringe from his eyes and hawklike nose, to salute the great god, pulling out a few eyelashes and hairs from his eyebrows and throwing them with kisses upward to the divinity in heaven. Effective, no doubt, even though they might land in the baggage rack. Then he would beckon for a refill of *chicha*, pouring a little in the aisle as a libation.

In the Lima airport I am sure the Inca would be at a loss, so we will leave him there. In any case he would soon disappear towards the parking lot to seek his gold litter and his eighty-two Rucana bearers, the "feet of the Inca," who would take turns carrying him, four of them at a time, on the journey of many days from Lima to Cuzco, through forests, over mountains, across the huge suspension bridge over the Apurimac River, arriving finally at the capital of his kingdom of Tahuantinsuyo, Royal Cuzco, the center of the Four Corners of the realm — Cuzco, the Navel of the World.

***

All modern airports are confusing, but Latin American ones have an added turmoil, a St. Vitus' dance of activity leading nowhere."The–flight–to–Cuzco–from–this–gate...no–no–from–that–one...it–is–delay–ed...it–has–gone...it–is–full...your–ticket–is–for tomorrow...you–used –it–yesterday...yes–it–says–reconfirmed–but–we–never–heard–of–you ...check–in–every–twenty–minutes–at–this–desk ... in a–few–hours–something–may–turn–up ... if–you–go–to–the–bathroom–we–will–leave–without–you...if–not–you–will–stand–here–indefinitely–shift–ing–from–foot–to–foot."

There are no people in the world who look at the clock as often as travelers from the United States. We imbibe punctuality with our mothers' milk and continue it with the time clock, the schedule, the division of the day hour by hour. We do not consider this odd; it's the way our lives are compartmentalized. Other countries may encourage a different view, with emphasis on the important leisurely lunch, the understandable delay to look at a sunset or call a friend.

There are many Latin American jokes about time.

"Meet me at 8:30 tomorrow morning. We'll have breakfast in the restaurant together."

"Sorry, I can't do that."
"Why not?"

"It's too early. I can never get anywhere by 8:30 in the morning."

"That's all right. I can't get there either."

In Arequipa a Peruvian chauffeur explained to me that Mexicans may be behindhand, but Peruvians haven't even checked the clock.

"We're that way," he said, proudly I thought, "but you Americans are something else. You insist on punctuality, but why do you do it both ways?"

"What do you mean, both ways?"

"I drove an American and his wife to the Canyon de Colca and he was very angry because I picked them up five minutes late. *Five minutes!*"

"I know," I said humbly, "but what do you mean both ways?"

"The next day I got up, skipped my coffee, forgot to say goodbye to my children, drove dangerously through the streets, and arrived at the hotel. The gentlemen was angry again. Because this time I had arrived five minutes early."

So how can I complain about the hours spent in the Lima Airport where, incidentally, I have made delightful new acquaintances and cemented old friendships, while everyone I have ever met in Peru gathers in the lounge to await developments.

"The–plane–couldn't–leave–Iquitos–too–much–mud–on–the– field... late–again–the–pilot–dropped–off–a–bundle–in–Tacna...some–plane –trouble–over–there–in–Cajamarca ... flight – to – Miami –canceled– come–back–tomorrow..."

For the Incas time was not the same as it is for us. It did not pass, it was not fleeting. Nothing ever died or was forgotten. Time referred rather to the origin of all things, the *paccarik pacha*, "dawn time," the beginning of the world. Time mixed the ever-present past with the actual present and the future. Incas did not count the years although they followed a natural calendar of sowing, growing, harvesting, seasons of rain and dryness. The calendar of the months manifested itself in the waning and waxing of the moon, in harvest celebrations, based always on the fixed data of the immutability of Inca origins, a past which was itself time.

This was the theory of time, as it was understood by the Incas, but yet its passage did creep into man's thoughts as it always must. Pachacuti, one of the greatest emperors, recited his own death song:

> *I was born like a lily in a garden*
> *And even so as I raised to manhood;*
> *And when time came I grew old;*
> *And when I had to die I withered and expired.*

His listeners knew, of course, that he did not really die, that time did not really take any toll, for he would live forever as a mummy cared for as solicitously as in life. Nothing would vanish, nothing be forgotten.

I had waited in the line of passengers for Cuzco only a little while when I felt a tug on my sleeve. A pretty girl spoke to me in perfect English.

"You are with which tour?"

"I am with no tour." My answer was in Spanish for I don't like to speak my own language when abroad, if I can help it. "I prefer to travel alone."

She shook her head. "You are not alone now. My name is Alicia and you are with me. You should not be alone. You are a little older than some..." She patted me on the shoulder, removing with this affectionate gesture a decade or two. "I will help you board, and you will be met in Cuzco by my agency." Travel agencies in Peru are as numerous as llamas on the altiplano.

"What will that cost?" I asked suspiciously.

"Just ten dollars, Señora, and you will be taken directly from the airport to your hotel, if you have reserved a room. If not we will help you."

"Ten dollars!" I cried, outraged. I haven't lived for years in Mexico without learning a thing or two. I struggled to free my arm, picked up my bag, turned away.

Alicia's voice was gentle, understanding. "Of course," she said quickly, "For you, Señora, it will be two dollars." She slapped a round yellow decal onto my sweater. It said "Inti-ito Tours, the ones who care" in several languages. I left it there and allowed Alicia to watch my things while I went to the bathroom.

As I joined her again a small group of young men in shorts and bright cotton shirts erupted from the arrival gate. They carried bows and arrows and long black blowguns.

"What's that? The guerrillas? The Sendero Luminoso?"

Alicia laughed. "No, Señora Celia, the Sendero Luminoso are surely better armed. Those are tourists coming back from the jungle trip to Pucallpa."

A young American loped by me, his blowgun at the ready. I had an instant mental picture of a U.S. newspaper headline: PERUVIAN PLANE HIJACKED BY AMERICAN WITH BLOWGUN.

Alicia read my mind. "The attendants confiscate them during flight. No danger." Her voice sank to a hiss. "Souvenirs, Señora, just souvenirs. Americans always want them."

I waited impatiently, forgetting once and glancing at my watch, for the overdue flight to Cuzco which would take only an hour or so this morning.

"Now boarding for Cuzco. . ." Alicia handed me my carry-on bag, I always keep the camera pouch slung over my shoulder, and patted me tenderly again on the arm. "*Buen viaje*. The Inti-ito Tour will meet you at the airport, and for only two dollars, for *you*. . ." She was still gesturing encouragingly as I went out onto the field and followed the crowd towards a plane waiting, with its boarding ladder extended invitingly.

***

Through Alicia I met Eber, who was to accompany me for ten days. I had not planned such luxury but my camera bag was my downfall. The Inti-ito agency chief met me at the plane and Eber, his driver, offered to drive me around for sightseeing and photography every morning for the next few days. The price was reasonable, Eber a pleasant young man. "I speak some Quechua," he said, and that decided me. It was Sunday.

"We'll start Tuesday morning," I said. "Until then I'll just walk around the city, taking pictures wherever I find them.

"Not with that bag!" Eber and the chief cried in unison. "You'll never make it back to the hotel with that." I inquired in the hotel and found that they agreed. No valuable looking equipment or I would be the natural prey of the thieves and pickpockets who infest the Royal City of Cuzco these days.

Mancio Sierra de Leguisame, conquistador, wrote: "The Incas governed in such a way that there was not a thief, not a criminal not an idle man. . .The Indians left the doors of their houses open, a stick crosswise in front of the door as a sign that the owner was not in... and nobody would enter."

Times have changed. I take the modern malefactors on faith, for I have never met one, thanks to Eber. They do exist. It is said that 80% of visitors to Cuzco are robbed, giving it the runaway lead over Bogotá where earrings and glasses are removed from travelers as they pass through the airport. Without my camera bag I went safely alone everywhere. Plunder, not mayhem, was in the air.

The Cuzco Valley was described in loving detail by Garcilaso de la Vega, the half-Inca, half-Spanish chronicler: "The valley, in this spot, is perfectly flat, and surrounded on all sides by high mountains; it is watered by four small streams and, in the center, flow the waters of a beautiful spring ... the land is fertile and the air could not be healthier; the climate is more cold than not, without it being so cold that one must have a fire to keep warm; it suffices to shut out drafts to forget the cold out-of-doors; if a brazier is lighted, well and good, but if there is none, one doesn't miss it. The same can be said about clothing and beds; winter clothing is bearable, but one can well get along without it, and people who like to sleep with only one cover, sleep well, and those who like three do not suffocate either."

Garcilaso also reported that everyone visiting Cuzco, when drawing close to the city, exclaimed, *"Najay tucuyquin hatun Cossco,"* "I greet you, great city of Cuzco."

Looking down on the city of Cuzco

Juan de Acosta wrote: "As if it were a holy land there were in Cuzco more than 400 shrines. Every place in it was full of mysteries."

Its streets were laid out at right angles, paved down the middle with a gutter for water, of a width that only one horse and rider could go on one side of the gutter, and another on the opposite side. The Holy Square held the palaces of the Incas — each new ruler built his own — and the Convent of the Virgins of the Sun. On the banks of the Huatanay River was built the splendid Temple of the Sun with its golden garden.

As soon as I arrived in Cuzco I felt an exhilaration which was to accompany me all through the high country. Cuzco is at 10,000 feet and the altitude was a heady draught, reinforced at the hotel by a draught of *mate de coca,* tea of the coca leaves, which is believed to prevent heart problems in high places. No hotel in Cuzco would be without it, and every guest is offered a steaming cup which one drinks seated in the lobby before being shown to his or her room. Although cocaine is made from the coca leaf, in its tea form coca is not strong, no more stimulating than a cup of ordinary tea. I felt exhilarated but never suffered bad effects from the altitude, perhaps because in Mexico I already live at over 6,000 feet, and my blood has become accustomed.

Just as the sun reached its zenith I set out alone, without my camera bag, for the Plaza de Armas, the great square known to the Incas as *Haucaypata,* Leisure Square, the heart of Inca life.

What I saw, when I entered the Plaza de Armas from the side street, was a beautifully designed, very Spanish main square, with arcades around the sides, a cathederal with scaffolding in process of being strengthened against earthquakes, a particularly handsome Church of the Society, which I knew to be resting on the remains of the great Amaru-Cancha palace of Inca Huayna Capac. The buildings are not all uniform white; some are in shades of blue or rose, reflecting softly the sunshine.

The crowd in the square this Sunday was typical: a brass band in one corner playing lively tunes, a group of businessmen on benches reading the Sunday paper, little girls in frilly dresses playing tag and small boys kicking a soccer ball.

Through the square walked an Indian woman, *campesina,* wearing a many-layered skirt, and shawl, in various bright colors, with a white top hat perched on her black hair. The shawl held a small baby on her back, staring out from under a wool cap. She was bent on some errand. She walked straight ahead, perhaps going to the market, without wasting a glance on her surroundings. She did not smile. She and the baby seemed to be wrapped in memories of some life that used to be long before they were born, but of course that is a sentimental imagining on my part.

In any case there was a different group of Indian women seated under the archway at the corner, with sweaters and ponchos laid out for sale. Their babies, swaddled or crawling around, stayed close to where their mothers squatted. This group was vociferous, urging their crafts on passing tourists. Cuzco, no longer the center of the world, is still one of the biggest centers of South America for foreigners: tour groups, archaeologists, anthropologists, students of weaving, and the perennial hippie, the "Jippi" finds in Cuzco the perfect answer—the acme of unbourgeois living and possible contact with an ancient spirit world.

The usual commercial projects go on under and behind the arcades: pharmacy, pizza parlor, money changers, travel agents, "typical" clothing stores with embroidered blouses, alpaca sweaters, Inca-inspired pottery, small brass llamas carrying loads of small fake emeralds, and "regular" clothing stores with nylon shirts and frowsy skirts already ripping at the seams, along with panty hose and high heeled pumps.

A corner of Cuzco's main plaza

Looking across the plaza, still one of the most beautiful in the world, I imagined what it must have been like just before the Spaniards came, in 1530 say, in September, time of the *Situa* when most of the harvest was in and the celebration included purification and saturnalia. Beforehand all foreigners, all cripples, and all howling dogs were moved beyond a two league limit from the city. The moon mother presided at this festival, while warriors hastened from the four corners of Leisure Square, the navel of the world pursuing Evil in a relay race taken up by shouting soldiers until Evil had been swept all the way to the rivers at the edge of the province. At night, after shaking what remained of Evil from their clothing, the participants performed the *pancunco,* beating each other with straw torches which they then hurled to the sky, destroying malevolence of every sort. Next daybreak everyone bathed, cleansing themselves in sacred waters, each group in its own stream. After this people joined together in eating the sacred porridge of corn flour and llama blood. The Sun and his children were now again at one.

The following revelry was a time of perfect goodwill, when all were fed, only kind words were spoken, beautiful clothing was worn, and sexual license reigned. After four days of celebration the mighty city of Cuzco permitted foreigners to reenter and join in the festival. They danced before the Emperor and he bestowed gifts. Again, by this means, the Empire was joined with outlanders from far away participating and becoming one with the Inca and his chosen people.

At its zenith Cuzco was a city of 200,000 people, divided into four residential quarters. Inhabitants from territories which had been absorbed into the Empire lived in sections corresponding to their geography. Unquestionably, it was the greatest city in the universe. Recognizing this, an Indian going into Cuzco stood aside when he met an Indian leaving it. Outlying districts had fanciful names: "silver serpent," "place for talking," "puma's tail." Cieza de Leon wrote of Cuzco that it "evinced a manner and a quality of greatness; it must have been founded by a people of exceptional presence." The Incas themselves called it *Topa Cuzco,* Royal Cuzco.

The dozen different races living in the city center were recognizable by their different head-dresses, a practice which is sometimes still followed today. Citizens of Pisac, for instance, can be easily recognized by their fringed hats. In the old days in Cañari from Quito-way wore their hair twisted around their heads under wooden crowns; the Cyanchis wore wide head bands; the Anti stuck bird feathers in their hair; the Urcas lurked behind fierce masks. All were separate but all were together, accountable to the Inca, direct, divine representative of the Sun. He ruled them in a for-the-most-part-benevolent dictatorship.

The Square was a cosmopolitan scene, not only in its inhabitants but in its goods and services. All roads led to Cuzco just as all roads had led to Rome, a city which it resembled in many ways. Sea shells arrived from the coast, coca from the East, bird feathers from the jungle. The store-houses of the Inca were jammed with fruits of the realm; salt, dried meat, cotton and wool, dried fish, sandals, hummingbird feathers, tools for workmen, gold and silver vessels for household use. There were "man-drums" made from the stuffed skins of enemy warriors, memorializing, pleasantly for the Incas, the conquests which had made them lords of everything their world could provide. They had a Quechua song for the darker side of their activities, the sorties to subdue new tribes.

> *We'll drink Chicha from your skull,*
> *From your teeth we'll make a necklace,*
> *From your bones, flutes,*
> *From your skin we'll make a drum*
> *And then we'll dance.*

Looking around this still mighty plaza what remnants do I see of the Inca past? Nothing but the monolithic stones which form foundations for Spanish houses. From the Christian place of worship are now streaming darkhaired ladies in short black dresses, their husbands in sober business suits, their children in clothes which indicate the care of nursemaids at home. Here come also the devout of lesser positions, the girls in cheap dresses from the "regular" dress shop, the young men in American style jeans. Turning my back to the church I look across the square where the gaggle of small boys is still kicking the soccer ball, and a couple of tourists are leveling cameras. Another Indian woman strides across the square, hurrying, her multicolored skirts swirling around her legs, her baby like a piece of her costume swaddled on her back. I don't know where she is going. Certainly not toward the cathedral. Perhaps she is heading

An old Indian woman walks across the square

toward the Temple of the Sun for the celebration of the *Situa*. No, of course not. She is followed by a dejected-looking black dog. Surely he should be beyond the two league limit while Evil is run out of town. Then so should I, for I am a foreigner here.

"Postcards, chicle. . ." A tiny boy tugs my arm. I shake my head. He brings out his master stroke, his word of English, "Mo-ney."

Festival of the Sun

It was in the Inca code of laws, all of which were always followed to the letter, that there should be three days of celebration every month, when no work was done and everybody rested. This was one rule that was easy to follow and there were so many rituals and special occasions besides — the *Inti Raymi*, the winter solstice in June, the festivals celebrating planting, harvesting and other natural events, that the common people must have been kept too well entertained to brood on their rugged lives of physical labor. In this way too Cuzco followed Rome. No decisions had to be made, for Tahuantinsuyo was a socialistic, cradle-to-grave empire. All marriages were performed on the same day of the year between girls of eighteen and boys of twenty-two or twenty-three, everyone received his parcel of land, everyone paid his dues in produce or services to the Inca and the Gods, no one starved for the state kept plentiful reserve granaries. In case a community did not pay taxes in kind they were instructed to deliver to the Inca, a quill full of live lice." This presumably encouraged them to pay the necessary tribute.

The marriage of common people was performed by a mere exchange of sandals, but the wedding of an Inca was a three-months-long period of extravagant display of wealth and power culminating in dramatic ritual on the marriage day. The betrothed, who was the Inca's sister (a somewhat skeptical safeguard to insure purity of royal blood) prostrated herself humbly before her bridegroom. The priest poured bowls of chicha on the ground in the Temple of the Sun. Two pure white llamas were sacrificed. The Inca helped his bride to rise and gave her fine clothing. He took a golden sandal and slipped it on her right foot, while her hundred serving maids looked on. The Inca and all the nobles prayed, kissing the air and blowing hairs from their eyebrows up to heaven.

Perhaps the couple strolled in the Golden Enclosure beside the Temple of the Sun, the supreme-glittering-useless-extravagant symbol of wealth or rather, to the Incas, symbol of beauty for they had no conception of wealth. Gold and silver were mined and made into beautiful objects simply because they were beautiful. In fact, when the Spaniards arrived, rapacious for precious metals, the Incas could not understand it. Did the white men eat gold?

This Golden Enclosure, the *Curicancha*, was the most amazing sight the conquistadors saw in the Royal City. Its field was planted like an actual field but all in gold. Golden ears of corn appeared to grow naturally, golden tassels and all, on stalks of gold planted in clods of gold instead of earth. Golden lizards and frogs crouched between the plants, golden birds and butterflies perched on the boughs. Fruit trees, made lifesize in precious metal, dripped with silver and gold fruit. The chroniclers gaped at every wonder as they catalogued the unbelievable display. There were twenty golden llamas and their young, full size, with their herdsmen, all constructed of the sacred metal. The riches included golden grass and even golden weeds.

***

In two or three days I had accustomed myself to the altitude of Cuzco, although I still enjoyed a cup of coca tea now and then ... good for the heart, I told myself. Always I had Eber with me in the mornings when I carried the sought-after camera bag, but in the afternoon, when pictures had been taken for the day, I wandered the narrow streets and climbed the hills by myself. The people I met were divided between Spanish types who, even though usually *mestizo* (mixed blood), dressed and behaved like Europeans, and Indians in costume, speaking Quechua, minding the old ways. Through Eber I was able to talk to some of the latter, but they had a withdrawn dignity which forbade impertinent questions I would like to have asked: Do your children go to school? Are they learning Spanish? What do you think of this garish modern world which you have never joined?

At the Hotel Tambo where I stayed the price was reasonable, the employees friendly. The hotel specialized in tours for high school age boys and girls. In Peru, I soon found, when teenagers get away from home they distance themselves from civilized behavior immediately. A couple of fierce female dragons attempted, without success, to handle their charges. No visiting in the bedrooms, so the corridors became jammed with young bodies lolling against the walls, bending over the potted plants to embrace each other, turning up the volume

Llamas and their mistresses

of the tape decks. No use trying to telephone, the lines were all tied up with kids calling home to Lima for more money. Gone forever the classic picture of a demure Latin damsel in a ruffled white dress, sitting on a balcony, with her duenna beside her, and casting shy looks towards the suitor in the street below.

I went out to meals and amused myself with the English side of the menu. No one had edited it. Why not? For a bowl of soup I'd correct the whole bill of fare. Perhaps it is considered chic to offer a "hand sandwich," "chicken in pickpocket sause" (I never translated that one: a reference to the anti-social element?), an Istek Gorden Bluey, or Ente Cott followed by Plumb Kake.

Garcilaso de la Vega tells us, apropos of menus, "Once the Spaniards found a big cooking pot full of boiled meat . . .When all had eaten their fill, one of the Spaniards fished out of the pot a hand with fingers on it." This was another tribe of Indians; the Incas were not cannibals.

In the mornings Eber and I made our daily excursions, covering a different section of the Sacred Valley of the Incas each day. We required no retinue of obsequious bearers, such as those who always accompanied the Sapa Inca. When we had engine trouble Eber jumped out and proved to be a good mechanic, while I took pictures, of the river snaking through the Sacred Valley, of the mountains rising above us, and of the wayward llamas and their mistresses loping down from the nearest ridge to invite the picture-taking. In many parts of Peru children and grownups ask for photographs. The Polaroid is perfectly familiar to the Yagua Indians near Iquitos, and to the vendors waiting at the train station for the mob to descend from Machu Picchu.

I had no Polaroid so I could not provide prints. Whether for this reason or some other, the Indians who wandered down while Eber was fixing a tire, did not ask for pictures of themselves. They accepted *soles*, measured out in a miserly way to Eber with a word or two in Quechua, then stood stolidly, a llama sometimes resting his head on his mistress's shoulder—surely there was more communion than the usual one between human and animal.

During our days' excursions Eber and I saw churches, markets, farms, rivers, Inca ruins now carefully preserved. We saw women walking along spinning as they went, or sitting at the base of the mountain weaving blankets to sell to passing strangers. We watched communal threshing and stopped for a look at a corn-sorting establishment where the maize was put through a hand operated screening process to separate big from little grains. It was then put in sacks, white for large, black for the smaller kernels. We passed houses with red paper flowers on jutting flagpoles. "That means they have chicha for sale," Eber told me and occasionally, a white flower as well, "That means food." The roads were bordered with yellow flowers, a kind of heather, in full bloom, hummingbirds hovering among them. We stopped to look at a beehive oven, and to examine a plow so heavy it took six men to carry it.

A country woman stops for a chat

Some of the people we met, and the country people were always friendly, spoke a patois half-Spanish, half-Quechua so I could understand them partly. More often we had to converse by way of Eber.

There were few tourists to be met on these excursions for we started in time to see the sun beginning its slow progress up into the extraordinary blue sky, in which clouds had apparently been dispersed by an artist with instructions to move gracefully, not too fast and not too slow, across the heavens.

The Sacred Inca Valley was known to the Incas as *Cuzcoquiti*, the "region of Cuzco." Here the rivers came together to become the Huatanay, later joining the Vilcañota. The up-and-down country provided natural building sites for fortifications large and small. The valley was backed by the holy white-clad mountain, Apu Ausangate, near which our plane had flown when I arrived from Lima. In the cliffs of closer mountains were clefts and caves where Inca dead were buried, and on these mountain sides Inca descendants still till the ground in the old way, on *andenes*, terraces which have not changed in hundreds of years. They form a pattern of semicircular retaining walls supporting plots of arable earth which make the hillsides look, from a distance, like an architect's plan for a future housing development.

Mt. Ausangate & the Sacred Valley

There are many Inca ruins — at Pisac, Ollantaytambo, Puca Pucara, Chinchero. Most of these forts were built on the top of a hill or cliff, not easy to climb, especially when starting from a base at 10,000 feet or more. I wish that I had once come upon a ruin on the level. But of course that was unlikely. In Inca times such an edifice would have become a ruin the first time a hostile army came by.

Inca ruins in the mountains

A sacred Inca fountain

Everything in the Inca world was alive, sentient, the universe and all its contents sacred. There was no such thing as a dead object, whether stone, rainbow or river. The earth mother, Pachamama, was sacred above all, living, vital, giving or withholding crops. She must be treated politely as must all of nature. Before working a field the farmer spread coca and chicha on the ground to invite it to give crops. Before crossing a river he drank a little of its stream, asking politely that his crossing be sanctioned. He understood that a traveler should always place a stone, in homage, at the summit of a mountain pass. Today these stones, *apachitas,* are still there and in fact increase in size as true believers place a rock upon them. When Eber and I went on our morning excursions we too placed a stone here and there, Eber with some disdain, I with apology for profaning the pile with idolatrous fingers.

The ruins we visited were overlaid with a well-kept history. There was a zig-zag in one rock where, in Inca times, chicha had been poured to foretell the future. If the liquid flowed down the left gulley there would be a good harvest, if to the right, a bad one. At another place there were two stones to set foot on, where an Inca virgin had crouched to urinate — a good future if her urine reached a certain spot in the downhill grade.

The farmer of the Inca highlands was busy, raising more kinds of plants than were cultivated anywhere else in the world. Beside twenty varieties of corn, forty kinds of potatoes, there were sweet potatoes, beans, squash, avocados, peppers, with tropical fruits and coca leaves imported from the lower provinces.

Most famous of all ruins in the Sacred Valley of the Incas is *Sacsahuaman,* the "Spotted Hawk," popularly known by the name of the hill on which it was built overlooking Cuzco two miles away. The Incas called it *Intihuasi,* House of the Sun, their mighty fortress, their place of refuge, a secondary city to Cuzco. Facing eastward toward *inti llocsina,* the "place where the sun springs up," it was sacred to the dawn, for the sun touched it while the royal city was still in darkness.

It was not yet finished when the Spaniards came, although it had been seventy-five years in building. Cieza de Leon wrote later, "Even if their monarchy should have lasted to the present, it would still not have been finished." Twenty thousand workers labored there, 4,000 quarrying boulders, 6,000 dragging them on sledges to the site, others cutting poles, repairing cables, grinding the stones when they were in place. Said Cieza, "To set the base, they excavated down to the very rock; this they did so well that the foundations will remain as long as the world shall last." Up until now, at least, he is right, for the outer foundations are still formidably intact. The three walls of Sacsahuaman are typical of all such strongholds in Peru, but the fitted irregular boulders are the largest in the world. "Neither the stone aqueduct of Segovia nor the buildings of Hercules nor the work of the Romans had the dignity of this fortress," wrote Cieza.

Each of the three walls of the fortress was named for a section of the royal city, and within were three towers, the center one a special auxiliary palace for the Inca's use. It was a thatched castle with apartments for the royal women, baths, terraces, storehouses, a piped-in-supply of water. The Spanish estimated that the fortress complex could provide refuge for 10,000 people in time of attack. The Inca kept a permanent military force in readiness at the *Intihausi,* with a huge armory of bows and arrows, clubs and hatchets, shields, spears, quilted armor.

The building of Sacsahuaman went on for seventy-five years. When the Spaniards came its destruction was not nearly so laborious. After eight years of looting, transporting rocks for the construction of European-style buildings in the city below, the leadership of Cuzco forbade further use of the materials. In any case they did not have 50,000 workmen to remove the immense foundations, boulders weighing tons, intricately fitted together, and these remain for us to wonder at. As tourists we roam the hill of the Spotted Hawk, where the monuments of Inca empire stand for the camera and llamas gather with their owners to have their pictures snapped against the background of history.

The llamas of Sacsahuaman appear to meet the tourists, on weekends only, pose daintily for photographs and watch as their owners collect the fee. Their expression says: "More than that. Come on, haven't you heard about inflation?"

Like everyone else who visits Peru I was entranced by the llamas, at least most of them were llamas. There were actually four different animals: llamas, alpacas, guanacos, vicuñas. The guanacos and vicuñas, however, live in the very high reaches, keeping a fleet-footed distance from man, their long necks curving like swans, their delicate hooves galloping over the wastes of the altiplano. Alpacas are heavier furred than llamas, their wool the preferred material for sweaters and ponchos.

The llamas were referred to by the Spanish chroniclers as sheep, which they could not have been — the Indians had no sheep. They were not an ordinary animal and showed it, as they still do, by their demeanor. In essence the llama is, as Father Cobo said, "the only animal which domestication has not degraded, for it only agrees to be made use of when asked, and not when ordered."

The conquistadors were impressed with the llama; the Incas considered the animal sacred. The principal stars,

"Pancho of Peru" —photo by Gerald Charm

in the Pleiades, the Milky Way and the Southern Cross were identified as heavenly llamas. It was good luck to bury a llama fetus under one's house, and at least a hundred of them were sacrificed for worthy causes every month in the great square.

We get our information in dribbles from the conquistadors' accounts. From them we learn that llama paddocks were high for they can clear lofty obstacles at one bound, though one never sees a llama at large proceeding at more than a dignified pace. They cannot, or will not, carry more than eighty pounds of burden, less than a man can handle if he is a stout Indian. Their flesh is not fit to eat after three years of age because the meat absorbs a bitter element from the herbs they feed on.

Llama herds were an important part of Inca economy, totalling hundreds of thousands, and the Royal Inca knew the precise number of them. The punishment for the unauthorized killing of a female llama, when not part of a royal hunt, was death. Llamas were chiefly employed as cargo carriers, in war or commerce. A single convoy might total as many as 25,000. They could travel about twelve miles a day. Man could outlast any animal in the up-and-down world of Peru, could carry more than a llama and go longer distances; the labor was shared between man and beast.

The original llamas were believed to have issued from the bowels of the earth along with the Incas, after the mythical flood. The sacred Napa, a spotless white llama, symbolized Cuzco. His ears were decorated with gold ornaments and two maidservants, *mamaconas*, walked beside him in processions as he paced with the slow, disdainful movement of his kind. The Napa was trained to drink chicha and to munch coca leaves. At death he went to join his fellows among the stars in the pastures of the celestial *puna*.

One day I went to Machu Picchu by train. I invited Eber along, buying his ticket, for in all his thrity-five years he had only made the trip once to see the greatest ruin of all.

Eber was a *mestizo*, college educated, informed in history, but he showed and felt the traces of Inca blood. His father was of a family famous for its woodcarving and perhaps Eber should have followed in his trade, for his engineering degree could not get him a job in modern Peru where unemployment is running high and inflation higher. He drove his ancient Ford as a taxi to the airport, or on tours such as mine, and tried to support his wife and two children against increasing odds, for the older boy had some rare disease which required laboratory tests every few days. There was no goverment help to pay for it and Eber wore a harried look always. I paid him by the hour and we never exceeded the speed limit, creeping home sometimes at a snail's pace to make the extra half hour tariff.

A special train takes tourists to Machu Picchu, or at least to the station 2,000 feet below the summit on which the ruins stand. The train leaves Cuzco in the morning at about 7:30 and makes the station at 11:00. Passengers then crush through the exits and hurl themselves, as though fleeing from an enemy, at the minibuses which wait outside. It is a moment of tremendous, senseless excitement, since on reaching the site no one enters the place except in a group with a guide, and that means waiting for the late arrivals in the follow-up buses. However, after perhaps years of anticipation of seeing one of the the world's greatest monuments, the pressure is too great. To sit for a quarter of an hour waiting at the station is beyond imagination.

If anyone has ever entered Machu Picchu without amazement and awe, I have never heard of such a person. The fact that almost everyone has seen pictures and read descriptions makes no difference to the supreme moment. Not only are the ruins a magnificent, long-gone city, a place of memories, but the Incas built their aerie in a great location, as though envisaging the thousands of visitors who would, at this late date, visit their city.

Machu Picchu is on a saddle between two lofty, abrupt peaks, Machu Picchu (Old Picchu) and Hauyna Picchu (Young Picchu), and it is entered by a single narrow gateway, easily defendable in case of hostile attack. Within, it spreads out into a complex of terraces, houses for the nobility, lesser dwellings for the common folk, all dominated by a stone shape which may have been an enormous sundial. The thatched roofs disintegrated hundreds of years ago, but the stone walls, ponderous, intricately fitted, will remain in place indefinitely. A small government-run hotel stands close to the city entrance, effacing itself in a suitable way against the mighty historic backdrop.

Machu Picchu

There may be hundreds of people at a time wandering through the city-fortress, led by guides telling the story in Japanese, German, French, English, or Spanish.

It was September, out of season for tourists, when Eber and I visited Machu Picchu but passengers crowded the narrow gauge cars for the leisurely trip from Cuzco at 10,000 feet altitude to Machu Picchu at 8,000, crossing higher passes on the way. Switchbacks on the line are so sharp that the little train must negotiate every other level in reverse as it climbs out of Cuzco. Later it descends to run beside the fast-rushing Urubamba River, headwater of the Amazon. Precipices hem in the river valley while 20,000 foot snow-covered peaks form a backdrop in the distance.

Machu Picchu was discovered in 1911 by Hiram Bingham, searching for the "Lost City of the Incas." He worked his way through the jungle along primitive cliffs, always with the danger of meeting hostile

Ruins of the ancient city

Indians or poisonous vipers. Finally, "in the dense shadow, hiding in bamboo thickets and tangled vines, appeared here and there walls of white granite ashlars." He had come upon the Inca city in, as he wrote, "the most inaccessible corner of the most inaccessible section of the central Andes."

Some years ago the Peruvian government blasted out a river road and now it is an easy morning's train ride to the ruins. For the adventurous the Inca Trail enables hikers to reach Machu Picchu from Cuzco in a three or four day trek.

The routine at Macchu Picchu is to arrive at about eleven o'clock, have lunch in the cafeteria, take a guided tour, and leave again by bus at two o'clock for the descent to the station and return to Cuzco. Few visitors spend the night, but when I first went there with a couple of friends some years ago, we decided to stay over.

As soon as the crowd had gone the ruins became profoundly silent. Clouds, colored at evening by a pale orange and rose sunset, hung over range after range of mountains. The only sign of human life was smoke from *milpas*, fields being cleared by fire in the ancient way, on distant peaks. Looking two thousand feet down to the Urubamba River I grew dizzy. Later we returned from the hotel to climb the stairs and explore the paths by moonlight.

***

No one is certain, but perhaps Machu Picchu was the sanctuary of the Chosen Women. While we do not know details of life here, its use by the Virgins of the Sun is confirmed by the fact that nine out of ten of the skeletons recovered from the cemeteries are female.

Other such convents were described in early Spanish records. Girls were selected at an early age from among the best born and most beautiful, and consecrated for life to the service of the sun, the Inca, the nobles and the priests. They learned weaving, fine cooking, and the brewing of chicha. At sixteen a girl might become the mistress of an Inca, be married to a noble, or she might be chosen to spend her life in the sanctuary as a temple attendant and instructor.

The Virgins

In the ruins today no evidence exists of the daily life of the Chosen Women. The narrow-necked water pots which they kept by the basins of the Stairway of the Fountains, the kitchen utensils and the silver ornaments, have all been removed to museums. The mummies have been taken from their carved stone niches. Only ghosts remain.

What was Machu Picchu? Birthplace of the Inca Empire? A military outpost? Capital of Vilcabamba? An imperial retreat? Or, as Bingham thought, a refuge for the Virgins of the Sun? Eber and I discussed this as we ate a picnic lunch put up by the Tamba Hotel. We came to no conclusions. The lunch was made for teenage tastes: heavy peanut butter sandwiches, huge pieces of chocolate cake, Inca cola to wash it down. We sat on the edge of the cliff outside the ruins, between two eucalyptus trees, a thicket of yellow *retame* flowers at our feet. Bending a little forward, careful not to slide over the precipice, we had a view of the switchback road snaking down to the train station, 2,000 feet below, a toy at the river's bank where a torrent foamed impatiently over rocks. The little train was there too, waiting to start the return trip.

Eber and I agreed that we would never know what Macchu Picchu was in the time of its glory.

"It's enough that it is here," Eber said. "I am glad to have seen it a second time. It belongs to my people."

***

After ten days in Cuzco, where I could happliy have spent a year, it was time to move on to Bolivia which I had not visited in my two previous South American excursions. I went to the Aeroboliviana office and asked to reserve a seat for Tuesday. The girl looked up from her knitting — a blue afghan — and stared at me.

"There's no plane on Tuesday," she said, returning to her knitting.

"Any other day next week," I suggested.

She looked up again, made a face as though all should be obvious.

"No planes to La Paz next week," she said, adding, as an afterthought, "No planes ever."

"What happened?"

She bit her lip, having dropped a stitch, and shrugged her shoulders.

"Not enough passengers perhaps. Maybe hard to keep the planes in shape. There could always be a bomb around. Take the train to Puno."

I made arrangements to do so, relieved that this decision was forced upon me. The plane trip had been based on laziness, which I found increasingly governed my plans at 10,000 feet up. The train would be more trouble — overnight in Puno, changes, uncertain connections which seemed to be common at this altitude. However, I was happy to make this leg of my journey on earth with, at that height, the sky hanging close above me, to get a view of Peru and Bolivia not seen from the air. The section of the Royal Road from Cuzco to Puno and from Puno to La Paz can still give such a view.

I hurried to make my reservations on the daily train for the twelve or fourteen hour run to Puno and, through the same agency, to reserve a place on the bus, catamaran ship, and bus again, which makes the voyage-journey to La Paz. The agency, but then there are clusters of agencies all about, was said to have its office in the venerable luxury Hotel Cuzco. I went there, planning to have a Pisco brandy sour in the bar before making arrangements, just to get my courage up. Travel in the sense of actually moving long distances from place to place has always seemed a chore.

The bar was not near the desk where liveried elderly clerks stood hopefully in a red velvet setting. The Cuzco would not be heavily patronized at this time of year, off tourist season. However the bar was not empty. From it came a noise which reminded me of the teenage manic behavior in the Hotel Tambo. I went in, sat down without looking around, and ordered my drink. The waiter leaned close, "It's hard to hear you, Señora, did you order a Pisco sour?" I nodded.

***

The Transturin Agency, it appeared, had moved to the Plaza de Armas. I could easily find it but the doorman volunteered to escort me. "Why not, I have nothing else to do," he said frankly. "Not that we're not busy of course, but it's early in the day."

We set off, found our destination, and I was treated with the courtesy I always receive in Peru. Perhaps because I am old, perhaps because I am alone, perhaps just because they are Peruvians, these friendly people seem to adopt me at once. There was careful talk of when to start for the station, who would be assigned to accompany me to the train, consideration of the camera bag, bait for the malefactors infesting the station.

"You will arrive at Puno after dark, Señora. You must not. . . certainly no... get off the train by yourself with your belongings. Even in the station itself..." Eyebrows were raised, mouths pursed in disgust. "We'll call our agency manager there, give him your seat number, and he will come aboard for you. No, it's not too much trouble. For *you* it is no trouble at all."

"Is this really necessary?" I exclaimed, feeling like a piece of valuable baggage in transit. Next they'd be offering to carry me in a golden litter.

"Yes, it is necessary." The Hotel Cuzco doorman shook his head as he left me. "So dangerous. It didn't used to be this way. What will become of us? Poor Peru."

Poor Peru, yes, and beautiful Peru also, where everybody I have met has been friendly, dependable, honest . . . and the thieves, whom I fortunately have not met, are hiding inexorably around each corner.

My last day in Cuzco I spent nostalgically in familiar places. I went with Eber in the morning once more to look at Sacsahuaman. I took a few more pictures, for what if the others didn't turn out? This apprehension always haunts me since I never have any photographs developed until I reach home. This is based on sad experiences, and on the vagaries of Latin time as well. Once, in Quito, I went to the large Kodak office to inquire about making me some slides.

"Sorry, we can't do that. It takes a little time."

"But I'm going to be here in Ecuador a whole month."

"It takes six months. We send our negatives to Panama."

If I were an Inca, I thought, I would curry the favor of appropriate

Woven rugs festoon the square on market day

authorities to be sure my pictures are turning out. I'd toss a few eyelashes toward the sun, Inti, who in picture-taking is surely influential. Eber could stop at a chicha vendor's and we'd pour a suitable libation. There is no way, however, for a modern visitor like me to enter into the thinking of those early residents of the navel of the world. Science has spoiled it for me. I know what it takes to produce a good photograph, and only a little of it is divine favor. I know what the seasons will bring, give or take some drought or floods, but the Incas did not know that. Each year a petition had to be presented, and it is still true in these barren-looking fields today. How can a human being be sure, in the parched month of October, dry as it now is, that November will bring rain and December will pour torrents. The woman with her llama over there in the dry terrace may be reciting the old Quechua prayer still spoken at this time of year:

> *Pity my tears,*
> *Pity my anguish,*
> *The most distressed*
> *Of your children<*
> *The most distressed*
> *Of your servants*
> *Implores you with tears*
> *Grant the miracle*
> *Of water, your own,*
> *Grant the gift of rain*
> *To this unfortunate*
> *Person,*
> *To this creature*
> *You have created.*

In the afternoon, I sat for a while in the Plaza de Armas where I wondered if that over there could be the spot where the golden spike was sucked into the earth, signalling to Mama Ocllo and Manco Capac, on their journey from Lake Titicaca, that this was the navel of the world, the place to found their empire.

I looked up Loreto Street, imagining it as the Street of the Sun of Inca times, the route taken by the mummy-bearers in the grand processions.

Each royal mummy was attended every day by his personal retainers, who fed him, entertained him, whisked the flies from his face. He had, as in his lifetime, landed estates, coca fields, llamas by the thousands. As a mummy he was an *illapa*, a spark or flash of lightning, not a corpse like those of ordinary humans. In the grand parades he proved again that time did not exist, for no one or nothing ever really died.

Each mummy was carried in a litter trimmed with gold and roofed with shining feathers. He rode in a crouched position, staring sternly ahead at his people. Attendants bore his coat of arms, and held over his head an umbrella of brightly colored plumes and feathers, which gave off the aura of his living spirit, while the regal red fringe which used

Festival of the Dead

to cover his eyes, was carried by a special bearer. Even his tunic, coca bag, and sandals had their place in the procession.

Each mummy was accompanied by a *huaoqui*, a "brother" who had been his companion and auxiliary spirit in life. Manco Capac had a small dry Inti-bird in a basket, while his son chose a stone fish.

The mummies had "speakers" to do their talking, to call for food, drink, and coca to chew, to toast their fellow mummies in chicha and invite them to drop in for a visit at their palaces.

As I watched I thought the cortege entered the square, to the sound of singing and recitation. It marched around the perimeter of the plaza, each member finding his appointed place with the area surrounded by a golden rope. The celebration, in my mind's eye, now degenerated into a saturnalia, maybe the more vigorous ancestor of the Hotel Cuzco's modest celebration of pharmacists.

A church bell in the cathedral rang out, breaking up my imaginings with its Spanish clamor. Made from melted bronze and gold, it is said to be audible thirty miles away.

***

After the noise died down my mind skipped to another, terrible scene.

It was the year 1572. The Spaniards had burned the mummies; they had melted down the golden statue of the Sun God, Inti, to pay the debts of King Philip II. Francisco de Toledo was the Viceroy of the New Castile.

Uncounted thousands of Indians gathered in the great square of Cuzco to see the well-publicized execution of their ruler and god, Tupac Amaru, last of the Inca emperors. So many spectators came, and they made such a hubbub with their moaning and howling, that the Spaniards feared a riot. The Vicerory listened to the screams as he watched the scene from behind a curtained window.

The Emperor Tupac Amaru, a youth of fifteen, was led in on a mul dramatically caparisoned in black velvet. He calmly mounted the stage for his beheading. However, the cries of the Indians became so appalling that the frairs untied the condemned man's hands and asked him to quiet his people.

Tupac Amaru raised his right hand slowly, then brought it down. There was instant silence. The Inca had been baptized a Christian, and he made a speech somewhat as follows:

"My people, beliefs have been false. None of what you were taught was true. All was false. Inti, your God of the Sun, the God of your ancestors, never existed. Your God was, after all, only a lump of gold."

Tupac Amaru then placed his head on the block, the executioner cut it off with one blow and held it up. Church bells rang out while the Indian spectators shrieked and howled and groveled on the ground. They had lost their ruler, their world, and their universe.

All this happened in a Spanish city known as the Very Noble and Very Great City of Cuzco.

Every great square in every great city in the world has its past hanging in the air, heavy, sometimes menacing, sometimes alive with pleasure. No city center has more of this atmosphere than Cuzco, Tahuantinsuyo, the Holy City, the Four Corners where the world and the universe converged for a few years, only a moment's span in the history of peoples.

Machu Picchu—photo by Gerry Charm

***

Now I was back to reality. A small boy tugged at my sleeve. "Chicles? Chicles?"The girls perched on the other side of the fountain whispered and giggled. The balloon man over toward the cathedral made a sale to a mother, who wrapped the balloon string around her baby's wrist. They both smiled happily as they wandered off towards the soft drink stand. Overhead the sky was blue -- at this season I had not seen it otherwise — and the clouds performed their usual pirouette across it. I wished I could see a condor.

I headed back across the square to my hotel to pack for tomorrow's train ride. One teen tour had left, but another had already arrived with the noise, selfishness and zest which tourists of that age exude.

During my travels I saw many modern Peruvians touring, the rich who could afford it. They heard the stories of the past of their own people, Indian and Spanish, and saw in their cities and in the Inca ruins a hint that while the past was dead it was not all dead. Some of it continued to live on, as the mummies lived until they were burned.

Even when the mummies were destroyed, their "brothers," Inti-birds, stone fish, or formless rocks, carried the spirits. I wonder if the Viceroys thought to have all the *huaoquis* done away with? I thought that some might be wandering even today, waiting to hear the wails of their followers reverberating in the cañons and gullies of the Sacred Valley.

Eber drove me to the train. He arrived to pick me up at the hotel with Hector, his little boy, on their way to the doctor and the laboratory for yet another test. There were tears in his eyes as he left me at the station, delivering me into the capable hands of Rosa from the agency office. The tears were partly, of course, for the ending of a business arrangement which had held off financial disaster for another week or two, but I think they were partly because we had enjoyed our trips together, Eber learning something of photography, I something of Peru. He handed me a farewell gift, a meticulously carved wooden sculpture of an Inca, created by his father. I gave him a contribution towards inevitable medical expenses.

As Eber left the station, with Hector on his shoulder, to get to their appointment at the doctor's office, he turned and waved to me. Hector waved too, and grinned.

Machu Pichhu— photo by Gerald Charm

On the way to Taquile

A small stone statue from Tiahuanacu.

BOLIVIA

Fresh Fried Truth

•La Paz
•Puno
•Taquile
•Lake Titicaca
•Chacaltaya
•Tiahuanacu

Here the altiplano, desolate, enormous, colored from tan through ochre to dull copper and rich brown, stretches far away. And here at Tiahuanacu not even the name of a mighty ruler is remembered. When the conquistadors arrived the Aymaras passed on only the legend that the buildings had been created in a single day. Even in the last century some explorers believed this to be the lost Atlantis, and the starting point of civilization.

I climbed into the train, settled my baggage on the rack and myself on the comfortable buffet-car seat which faced across the table to an opposite bench. I introduced myself to Marge and Helen, art historians from the United States, studying on grants in South America.

They planned to get off before Puno, at Juliaca, to see some pictures in the church there. They were loaded with equipment: six suitcases, a bundle of books, medical supplies, a basket of emergency food, a tape recorder to note things of interest. We had a pleasant day together but after a few hours we ran out of conversation. They were on a serious scholarly mission, with much to discuss. Their talk was mysterious to me, since I don't know a phylum from a symbiont, or a tenon from a quern.

I was glad to have only my cameras and overnight bag to worry about, but looking at other people's things I felt a bit deprived just the same. When Marge asked me my object in traveling to South America, I had to think a minute.

"Just to look around," I said finally, feeling foolish.

The train, groaning and grumbling, meandered slowly upward out of the city. I looked through the dusty window at the receding tile roofs below me, and thought of Eber's Quechua aphorism: "A window is a hole that sees."

Again I noticed, as I stared out the window, that the sky seemed to hang close above the earth. We must already be over 11,00 feet and would climb higher before reaching Puno. On the first stretch the landscape was familiar. I had grown used to it in my day trips with Eber: the dry October terraces perched on the hillsides waiting for the rains. The Quechua rain prayer might not be enough. Other Inca ceremonies would have to be added, a beating of dogs and llamas, for instance, so that they too would howl for rain. Eventually the Gods would answer with rain and more rain, probably torrents. Meantime a few compesinos and herds of sheep plodded wearily across the dry fields and along the rough roads which crisscrossed the hills. Eucalyptus, originally imported but now prolific here, bordered by pastures, barrel cactus and maguey outlined the fields. The yellow broom, color of the divine Sun, was still in flower. We ate an early lunch of fruit cocktail, broiled chicken with rice, and beer. My table mates told me what to expect in Bolivia.

"I was sick in bed for a week there," Marge said, *"soroche,* that's mountain sickness, but you won't be. You're already acclimated. I made the mistake of flying straight up from Miami to La Paz."

"You'll like the country," Helen told me. "The people are kind. They don't rob you. It's cheaper than Peru too. Everything is a special price."

"What do your mean?"

"You'll find out when you get there."

After the valley of Cuzco the altiplano was another world. Chocolate-brown adobe houses rose like excrescences here and there from the barren brown land. From each house rushed a smallish black sheep dog to charge the train, following it, barking furiously, until it removed itself from his territory. At rural stations Indians in native dress, speaking Quechua more often than Spanish, hawked food and handcrafts. Small boys pursued the train eagerly, seeking to hold it long enough for a few *intis* to change hands.

Not so long ago, in the extended view of time, the scene would have been different. No metal houses on wheels with humans trapped in them proceeding noisily to a distant destination. Nobody around here had ever heard of the wheel. The Inca Royal Road came this way, extending 3,500 miles from Ecuador to Chile, with animal and human traffic all on foot, and the highway structured accordingly, in some places twenty-five feet wide and paved, in others a narrow mountain track or a series of stone steps, in still others crossing over rushing rivers on bridges made of woven reeds strong enough for a detachment of Incas and their llamas to pass together. The convoys traveled only about twelve miles a day, and at those distances, along the whole length of the highway, were *tambos,* or inns, for use of the Inca and his retinue. Each one was always fully furnished with food, equipment, clothes, for the Emperor never wore the same outfit twice, never ate twice from the same dish. Each Sapa Inca, during his reign, made a circuit of his kingdom from time to time, the journey taking months.

The royal approach along the highway was heralded by *chasquis*, professional runners specially assigned for relay marathons. Each youth had a piece of road about two miles long which he knew by heart and could navigate at top speed day or night. The service continued at all times, to keep the Inca fully informed of provincial affairs, and to take his bidding to distant places. It was said that he knew, not only of revolts that might be brewing, but of the exact number of inhabitants of his realm together with llamas and their young, and equipment, crops and possessions, down to the last pair of sandals on the feet of the last citizen to be counted.

the quipu

Two *chasquis* lived together, during their fifteen day stretch of duty, in a round hut by the highway not too far from their regular homes. They took turns at sentry duty, listening for the sonorous conch shell trumpet blown by an approaching *chasqui.* No time was wasted in stopping to deliver messages. The arriving courier ran alongside his relief while the dispatch was handed on, verbally or by means of the knotted *quipu* strings used for statistical information. The Incas had no writing, depending on the talents of trained "rememberers."

The courier service operated on a twenty-four hour basis, covering up to two hundred miles a day. Discipline, as in all Inca life, was severe. It is unlikely that any runner dared stop for a gossip about secret messages or for a noggin of chicha.

Cieza de Leon who, in his seventeen years of travel, described everything he encountered, wrote of the Royal Inca Highway: "In the memory of man no highway is as great as this, laid through deep valleys and over high mountains, through snowbanks and quagmires, linking snow peaks with stairways and rest stops; everywhere clean swept and litter-free. With lodgings, storehouses and temples of the Sun... The Roman road through Spain and the others we read of were as nothing compared to this."

The Inca in his golden litter did not travel alone. Besides his Rucana bearers in their blue uniforms, performing a service reserved for them because their tribe was renowned for mountaineering, he had the usual quota of courtiers, soldiers and servants who attended any absolute monarch. He had more than a few women. Cieza says that when Huayna Capac left Cuzco for the north he "carried with him 2,000 women and left in Cuzco more than 4,000."

Four of the Inca rulers—Manco Capac, the 1st Inca: Sinchi Roca, the 2nd Inca; Inca Roca, the 6th Inca; and Pachacuti Yupanqui, the 9th Inca

On this rumbling train we were making a journey of about two hundred and fifty miles from Cuzco to Puno in from twelve to fourteen hours or longer, averaging a rickety twenty miles an hour. The *chasquis* could make eight so we rushed along more than twice as fast, but it didn't seem so. It seemed from time to time as though our train, the express to Puno, might lie down and give up the struggle.

We stopped for a while at a small station where Indian children ran up and down the length of the train platform in hyperactive salesmanship. Most were boys, but a few girls specialized in narrow many-colored woven belts, whose prices fluctuated madly. One girl, ten years old or so, was outstandingly pretty, a sure-fire beauty in a few more years. She was shy, her long black hair flowing on her slender shoulders, her large brown eyes with their heavy lashes demurely cast down.

I realized with a shock that this girl was an Inca, misplaced by hundreds of years. She could have stepped from the pages of Poma de Ayala's book with its awkward drawings — he was the only chronicler to picture for us the Incas of his time. She was short in stature, earnest-looking as though following carefully remembered instructions. Her forehead was broad, her nose hawklike, with angular cheekbones, her skin the color of light mahogany. The way she stood straight as she offered me a woolen sash, and the way she pulled her shawl around her showed that she knew already she was the prettiest girl in town.

"What is your name?" I handed out through the window too many *intis* in return for a belt.

"Maria." She smiled and we had for a moment a flash of emotional contact, a sense of comradeship. This girl would grow up to match her promise of beauty; she would probably stay in the town (Sicuani I think it was) with her family and neighbors, marrying and living the life of her ancestors in the extended communal settlement, the Inca *ayllu*.

Even in this century she might follow the Inca life style as it was pictured by Poma de Ayala, working with her husband as he plows with a digging stick and she breaks up the clods for planting. In country places there have been few changes. Crops of potatoes and quinoa still round out the tally of the seasons and the years. In such a picture, Maria would have a baby on her back. As I thought this, she pulled the shawl, woven in shades of scarlet and earth-brown, tighter around her shoulders and turned to try for other sales along the train.

In the time of Inca rule, life for the potential beauty queen, Maria (whose name then might have been Star or Gold or Coca) would have turned out differently. With the national genius for organizing and systemizing, nothing in Tihuantinsuyo was left to chance. Beauty could not flower unseen. From time to time inspectors from Cuzco traveled though the empire, visiting villages, looking for pretty girls ten or twelve years old, physically perfect, intelligent, suited for a very special future.   Points of special beauty were rosy cheeks and light olive skin, but these were usually Cañar girls from the north. Maria, I noticed, blushed when she lowered the price of a belt, and her darker complexion would not put her out of the running (or save her if you prefer that thought), for her skin was clear and tawny. She could be counted on the *quipu* string records as one of the *pacco*, the "fair."

Certainly Maria would have been chosen. This would have meant for her a journey to Cuzco for four years of education in the craft of weaving fine fabrics, and chewing *mocca* to make fermented drinks.

She would enter the women's quarters, a dormitory where during her training she would be "someone always there and ready to help." She would learn to comb her hair with thorns set between two wooden sticks and put bark and beans in the water for her shampoo to make her hair "blacker than black" She would learn to pluck her eyebrows and use rouge of achiote berries.

Eventually Maria would appear before the Royal Inca to be told her fate, from which there was no appeal. She and all the other chosen girls were the property of the emperor, a form of tax levy, like ears of corn or puma skins.

There were several possible turns of fate for Maria. The height of luck would be to catch the Inca's eye and be invited to enter the palace, joining the mare's nest of intriguing women who surrounded him, bearing sons, fighting for favors for themselves and their offspring. Failing that, she might be given in marriage to a lord in a faraway city or as mistress or wife for one of the Cuzco courtiers, or be added to the pool of prostitutes. In times of emergency, chosen girls were occasionally sacrificed to bring about better times; Maria might be selected to end her short existence so.

Finally she might instead be assigned to spend the rest of her life as a virgin in the House of Chosen Women, tending the sacred *Coricancha* fire, serving the ever-living mummies and training girl novices. At the age of sixteen, her education finished, she would take up the life assigned to her. If she was allotted to chastity she must never deviate. If she did she and her seducer would be stripped, tied together, and hanged by their hair from the execution rock until they died. Their families would be hunted down and killed and their homes, no matter how far distant, would be razed. Perhaps, as she and her lover hung there, she would call out to the birds overhead:

> *"Take me with you, Father Condor. Guide me, Brother Falcon. Tell my mother that for days I have eaten or drunk nothing . . . Take my grief and my affection to my mother and father. Tell them what has happened to me."*

There were probably two or three thousand women, in various categories, living in the vast dormitory-palace in the center of Cuzco, isolated from the world but no doubt involved in rivalries and cliques. The *Coya Paca*, a female relative of the Inca, ruled the roost here, with twenty old men guarding the doors against exit or intrusion.

The chroniclers have told us about these arrangements, but we know few details. Since there was no writing we cannot hope to come across the memoirs of a Chosen Woman, but it is inevitable that a modern visitor should wonder about those fine points. Did her parents gladly give up the original Maria, happy for her noble future although they would probably never see her again? Did her less favored sisters resent her selection? Did her mother long to keep her at home ... to the extent of hiding her from the Inca's inspector (surely a perilous project) or leaving her hair uncombed, her clothes ragged and unwashed so she would escape attention?

At this point in my thoughts Maria came racing back along the platform to my window to make another sale. She had done well. Half the woven belts were gone. Now she set up a shrill cry, "Señora, barato, barato!" But it was too late to bargain and lower the price. The train gave a groan and a lurch, getting itself going like an arthritic old man. Maria ran beside it but we soon left her behind still calling stridently now, first in Quechua, then in Spanish, "Barato, barato! Señora!"

***

After more hours the way turned desolate. With only sparse vegetation, dwarf willow and alder, cactus and sage. Overhead clouds massed in a pale blue sky. Here, it seemed, any prayer for water might be unavailing. Herds of llamas stretched their legs to wander majestically through the open spaces. Men wearing knitted multicolored wool caps with earflaps guarded flocks of sheep, always one black sheep among the white. Vultures glided in a hopeful circle overhead. History says that the spectacled bear, the puma, the hairy tapir, once lived on the altiplano. This plateau between the two cordilleras of the Andes is a definition of solitude. Long ago travelers proceeded here with a minimum of talking lest they offend the winds.

Evening came down and we rattled stubbornly ahead, jouncing and groaning, over an uneven roadbed. Dogs still rushed from the houses, but the children had given up and gone home for supper. I thought of a Quechua verse which I had read somewhere, typical of the sad literature of a people of submission, a melancholy dating from the Spanish conquest:

> *Even a small dog, in the door of his house,*
> *Barks aloud.*
> *He waits for his master to caress him,*
> *And I, for no one.*

It was dark when we reached Juliaca, and Marge and Helen got down. We had discussed the perils of thievery. Their baggage was heaped on a carrying cart pulled by Helen. Marge slung a heavy leather bag over her shoulder. They would proceed straight through the station to a nearby hotel. After all, there were two of them, and it was only just dusk. I waved goodby from my train window as they disappeared through the station door. We'd meet later in Puno. And later on in Puno I learned that they were waylaid and reached their hotel minus one of the six suitcases. I was not sorry to be carrying so little impediments.

***

Puno is best regarded as a stopping place for a day or two to see the surrounding sights. As a city it is cold and unwelcoming but it is close to the lake. I am prejudiced in my memories of Puno, for there the legendary Peruvian hospitality wore thin. I had reserved a room in a decent enough hotel for three days but was ejected after one night in favor of a tour group, and directed to an "equivalent" lodging by the tourist agent. I later looked it up in the *South American Handbook* (the bible on Latin American travel if you can read very fine print.) The adjectives used to describe my hotel were ones I couldn't improve upon: "unfriendly, unhelpful, not recommended."

It was my first meeting with an "electric shower," a system whereby the wires from the water heater are attached directly to the shower head, with several possible results ranging from perilous to lethal. All guidebooks to South America mention this problem, with various suggestions including "keep your shoes on when you turn on the water." My solution would be to make the hotel manager handle the faucets. Since it was only for two nights, I went unwashed.

***

Lake Titicaca's fame is in its singularity as the highest navigable lake in the world. It is huge, 150 kilometers by 50, and up to 300 meters deep. The lake is fed by runoffs from snow on the Andes. It has only one exit, at the small river or Desaguardero, and is subject to disastrous floods along its shores. Quechua legend says that it was here on the Island of the Sun that the goddess Mama Ocllo lived, here Manco Capac, the first Inca, was created and from here he set forth to found the royal city of Cuzco, to be located wherever his golden staff sank of itself into the earth.

Uros women weavers

The Uros Indians live on the lake, on floating islands made from totora reeds. They are a separate race, not many of them left now, antedating the Incas and speaking their own language. The early chroniclers, Acosta and Herreta, wrote of the Uros, "When asked what people they were they replied that they were not men but Uros, as though they were another kind of animal."

***

Walking on a reed island is like stepping gingerly across a floating carpet. The islanders' crude huts are made from totora reeds, they fish from reed boats, and live an extremely primitive life. They have,

A reed boat under way

however, learned the benefits of tourism without which they could not survive. Bright woven strips of cloth are set out for sale. I encountered the Uros' savoir faire when I snapped their pictures. There was a price for picture-taking, of course, eagerly negotiated. I felt that these islanders would sell their souls for the right handful of *soles*, and they may well have believed they were doing so in a photograph. A lady with a ragged umbrella postured prettily, then snarled, "You owe me double. I saw you work that machine twice."

Around Puno excursions start from 12,000 feet up, and climbing ruins is only marginally worth it, at least to me. However, I was bent on seeing everything. Who knew when I'd be this way again. I must at least follow through on my statement to Marge and Helen, "I've come to look around." Other tourists seemed all to be young, most of them French, Swiss or Italian. They obviously hadn't hit thirty yet and had practiced their first steps on the Alps. I tagged along and made it to Sillustani, where huge *chullpas* or burial tombs, empty now, are outlined against the sky. No bodies in them, and no longer any treasure. The guide told us, smacking his lips a little, that originally they hadn't held only dead Aymara nobles (we were out of the Inca zone here) but also their women, entombed alive to keep their masters company. The Aymara, like the Incas, felt that death did not exist: the chief would continue in the other world and needed a good assortment of his usual attendants.

Aymara burial tombs

I sat on a boulder and rested. The guide entered into talk, examining my cameras with interest, and inquiring into my plans.

"This has been a hard day," I admitted, "altitude, you know. But tomorrow will be easier. I'm going by boat to Taquile Island."

The guide laughed. "Señora," he said, "if you got a little tired here I think it is unlikely you will reach the top of Taquile."

"I didn't know it had a *top.*"

"It's built like a pyramid, a natural one, and to get to the summit where the village is requires much climbing, no matter who does it." He waved a hand toward the Alpine youths.

"All right, this one I won't try. I'll stay with the boat and just take pictures along the shore. Please get the tour agency to put me up a box lunch."

Everything in the high country starts early, and the motorboat set out at six the next morning for Taquile. No place to get coffee beforehand, of course. There was a different guide aboard. He had never heard of my box lunch and I was doomed to choose between climbing to reach the fried fish served on top of this natural pyramid or spending all day without sustenance. We would arrive home late in the evening. I straggled along after the group.

My spirits were not raised by watching the native Taquile women bounding up the *grados*, the almost vertical steps, with heavy pottery water jugs strapped to their backs. Even the Alpinists wearied, stopping to admire the view of Titicaca far down below, but really to catch their wind. We reached the top at lunch time and, sure enough, these primitive islanders know their tourists. Everything was at hand — beer, soft drinks, French fried potatoes, fresh trout from the lake, a carefully hand-printed menu in Spanish one side, English on the other. I read the English side with interest and it was worth the climb because I discovered my favorite lakeside trout: in Spanish *trucha frita*, here in English "fresh fried truth." I tried some but, because of my exhaustion and the altitude, could only manage a forkful.

We descended by another declivity to where the boat waited. I looked down on the enormous bright blue enigmatic lake, where fresh fried truth is captured daily and where, perhaps, deep down, schools of finny prevarications swim lazily around.

On the long boat trip back to Puno the three boatmen took turns on the tiller, between times knitting themselves bright colored hats with earflaps. Knitting seemed here to be a masculine occupation. The only native woman on board lay perfectly still on the deck, her shawl wrapped tightly around her had, her five full skirts, all different colors, spread around her, so that she looked like a fallen flower which has passed its prime. She never stirred until we reached the shore when she got up quickly, wrapped her shawl around her shoulders, jumped onto the sand and disappeared down a path without looking back.

***

The journey from Puno to La Paz on the other side of the lake, first by bus, then changing to catamaran ship, and again on the Bolivian shore to bus, started early in the morning and ended long after sunset. The Quechua language of the Incas was rich in descriptions of nature, especially time and the weather: "coppery burning of sunset," the "time when the walls cast shadows," "spangled night," the "paling before sunrise." These phrases surfaced in my mind again and again.

The borders of the huge lake are shallow, a haunt of ducks, sandpipers and lapwings. At dawn men in reed boats were already busy fishing. A sailboat flitted before the wind, its reed sail straining. Islands were visible in the distance, though not Taquile, which was too far out. This morning the lake was an intense aquamarine blue, the mountains behind it stark white against a light azure sky with fluffy clouds — a whole palette in blue and white.

Our bus stopped for the modern border crossing. The road was paved on the Peruvian side, dirt on the Bolivian, revealing at once the poverty of this poorest of South American countries. A French tour group, two Italians, a couple from California, and I hurried to the main square to change Peruvian *soles* and *intis* for Bolivian *pesos*. Money was measured against U.S. dollars and the peso here was now about two million to the dollar. I decided to change three dollars worth of *intis*, just enough for taxi fare to my hotel in La Paz. It was Sunday, the *casa de cambio* was closed, but a small boy officiated at a card table in the square. It was littered with paper money, some of which had fallen into a hibiscus bush. The boy grabbed my *intis*, filled my fist with paper, and proceeded to the next customer. What did I get? The bus honked impatiently. After climbing aboard I spent my time figuring. Did I receive thirty cents, three dollars, or thirty dollars? Eventually I figured it out.

The forty miles of travel by boat showed to advantage the enormous array of white peaks across the intense blue of the lake . . . Cieza de Leon described travelling through the snowy regions: "Climbing great and rugged mountains, so lofty that their summits were lost in the clouds and the accompanying scud . . I was so done in that it was very difficult for me to reach the top and on turning to gaze down, it seemed that the ravines reached down into the bowels of hell."

On this boat trip I met an American traveler named Ben, a man well into his seventies who was finally acting out all the dreams he could not afford in his younger years. He had just been to the Amazon

Jungle, not your touristy places, but a camping spot where he and his wife spent a week fishing for piranhas, those little fish which would like to eat us but which, he said, are mightly good fried and eaten by people. He was now on his way towards the South Pole, hoping to join some expedition that had no age limit. His mind was on superlatives, places which he planned to see: Titicaca, the highest navigable lake in the world, La Paz, the highest capital city, its airport the highest capital airport. (He missed out on Chacaltaya, the highest ski run.) Later, he sent me a postcard from Tierra del Fuego, with penguins on it.

After disembarking from the catamaran we boarded another bus as spangled night came on, and traveled a winding road through a high, thin-aired plain. Suddenly the plateau terminated, showing the city of La Paz spread out in a bowl below, backed by the towering snow-fields of Mount Illimani. The highway was now paved. We descended at last into a valley filled with lights and traffic, a modern city dropped here, as though at random, in the middle of an ancient land.

On the sidewalk outside the bus station the stars above me had descended another mile or two. Looking up I felt myself among them, close to the sacred llamas and their young.

A taxi whisked me through the hollow of downtown La Paz. I had a reservation at the Hotel Gloria, above my usual budget at $35 a night, but worth it to rest after the long trip. Another charming, smiling brunette, with whom these southern countries seem almost over-supplied, greeted me at the desk, examined my passport, gave me a card to fill out.

"For one night only, probably," I ventured, thinking of the cost. "By the way, how much is the room?"

She tossed me that winsome smile — a name on her blouse identified her as Elodia — and disappeared into the inner office. She came back overflowing with human kindness. She learned conspiratorially over the counter. "For *you*," she murmured, "It will be $12 a night."

"I'll be here a week or ten days." I didn't ask her why for *me*, nor remark that I had met this phrase before. The Gloria was ful of guests, I had the last room, so it couldn't be financial famine.

I never figured out the reason but I do know that it wasn't my irresistible personality. It was a way of life. Other people have told me of the same treatment in other Bolivian hotels, even to the snobbish Plaza and Sheraton. for *you* it is always something special.

Before leaving the desk I showed Elodia the fistful of change, in worn paper bills, which the taxi man had given me. It was time to get some idea of the new kind of money.

"How much should I give the porter?" I asked, pointing to a boy who stood by the elevator with my bag.

Elodia took a couple of bills from my wad. "Give him this. A million pesos is about right."

I crawled into bed in the Gloria, a delightful hotel in every respect, after an unsuccessful effort to eat supper in the rooftop restaurant. Nothing wrong with the food; it was just that I couldn't eat it. A mouthful and I'd had enough. This lack of appetite stayed with me all of my three weeks in Bolivia and I happily lost ten pounds. I learned that other visitors couldn't eat either, a result of altitude. Also, when I had momentary sharp twinges in my jaw, I was told that the change in atmospheric pressure was making the fillings in my teeth contract (or maybe expand?) and I need not rush to a dentist.

In spite of these small inconveniences I relaxed comfortably in the rooftop restaurant, looking down into the streets at evidences of big city civilization: a huge flickering Toyota sign, cars inching along, their headlights flashing from the facades of highrise office buildings, the shrill clamor of whistles as traffic police curbed the impulses of impulsive drivers. The basin rim where the Indians live was a black line drawn with charcoal against the sky, separating the human lights below from the heavenly constellations just above.

No use trying to eat, and the waiter was not surprised to have me signal for him to remove my plate. I sat a while thinking idly that this would be a great place to start a fat farm. It would be easy for a smoker to quit too, because at this height it's hard to light a match or keep a flame going. La Paz doesn't even bother with a fire department.

***

The next morning I started with my camera to explore the city. All streets ran uphill, for the Gloria, along with other better establishments, was in the bottom of the large bowl. Later, on a city tour, I learned that the higher a Bolivian's social standing, the lower he lives in La Paz, since oxygen is at a premium. The president's mansion is a viewless gulley, while the poorest Indian climbs tortuously to the top of the cliff to live in an airless hovel with a heavenly view.

As I left the hotel no one cried, "Look Out! You'll be robbed!" I was approached but not by malefactors. As I rested on a bench in the Plaza de Armas taking a few photographs of the cathedral, a well-dressed man asked if he might sit beside me.

"I'm interested," he said, "because there are not many tourists in La Paz, and those who come usually arrive in tours and stay for three days only. Then they all move to the next destination where, I suppose, they can breathe easier. So I am wondering, Señora, what you are doing here alone."

La Paz' Church of San Francisco

My acquaintance showed not only interest in my projects, but a great knowledge of his country. This was true of all Bolivians I met; they knew their history, their inheritance of folklore and legend. They talked much less easily about their present era and its economic trials My friend gave me from memory a list of paperback books on Bolivia to be found at the Amigos del Libro bookstore, and a short rundown on early tales of Potosí and the lake which still swallows people. Then he said goodby and I went down to the bookstore, happy with this meeting.

Later in the day I sat on a bench on the Prado (its real name is 16th de Julio), a modern thoroughfare bisecting the city, with smartly dressed people strolling and, among them, a scattering of campesinos in their costumes, bowler hats set jauntily on the women's hair. I took up my camera for some views of traffic in this city center. A middle-aged woman, carefully dressed, immediately sat beside me, all curiosity. We talked, moving quickly to the subject of her home town, Sucre, where I planned to go in a few days.

"You'll love Sucre," she cried. "It's a beautiful city, lower than La Paz, easier than La Paz, friendlier than La Paz. Also it's Paris."

"Paris?"

"Yes . . in its little way. In Sucre everything French is admired. Students at the University study French rather than English, there is a French Cultural Institute, and the park has been designed to be a tiny Paris with a small exact copy of the Arc de Triomphe, and another of the Eiffel Tower, and you'll find the Champs Elysée on a child's scale. Sucre. . . You will love it."

What to do in the evening? After a rest at the hotel I consulted my city map and went out, turning resolutely up hill towards the Municipal Theatre, stopping every few feet to pant like a dog. Having made it, I collapsed on a bench in the small square across the street and considered the sign which read, "TONIGHT, *La Casa de Bernardo Alba*, by Garcia Lorca, ALL START CAST." I sauntered into the theater to buy a ticket, but it was only six o'clock, the show was at eight. The cashier directed me to a small coffee shop in the lobby. Coca tea and plenty of it. The woman who brewed my tea told me that she was the theatre manager's wife, joined me, and we chatted companionably.

"I hope you don't mind my being here for a while until show time," I said, realizing that there was a limit to the coca tea I could reasonably drink. "It's too far to go back to my hotel."

"It's almost two hours until we open. Where *is* your hotel ... The Gloria? But that's only three blocks down hill."

I nodded, still gasping from my climb, and she patted my shoulder solicitously. "We who live here forget."

The play, produced in stark black and white, with the tragic parts played to the full and a little beyond, somehow suited what I felt to be a stark landscape, though I hadn't seen much of it tonight. The man next to me made a running comment, showing interest in where I came from and what in the world I was doing by myself in La Paz, Bolivia, watching a community theatre production of Garcia Lorca. I explained.

"I'm here," he said, "but only because we have a shortage of top class productions. Garcia Lorca! All passion and no real feeling! The curtain rose on the last act before I had time to answer.

***

After a couple of days I was able to climb the sides of the La Paz dish, feeling always like an insect working its way up out of a trap. The Indian section on top was a continuous market, with everything for sale or barter. Sheets and pillowcases, boots, canned peaches, crocheted baby jackets, plastic buckets. I needed none of these things but was tempted to buy simply because the vendors looked so wistful.

The Street of the Witches, down nearer the center of town, attracts tourists, whom the witches greet with shrill screams of pleasure as they offer for sale small stone images of the earth mother, the Pachamamas, and allow the photographing of their necromantic llama fetuses — foot-long undifferentiated objects which, fortunately, did not remind me at all of the handome living creatures. The fetus is most effective, the witches claim, if it was a natural miscarriage; for it loses much of its power through artificial abortion.

***

"Not sure you can make it to Chacaltaya," the travel agent told me, although he was willing to provide a car and guide. "At 17,000 feet you may have problems." I pointed out that I had had no attack of *soroche* in my travels in the high country, explaining that this might be because in Mexico I live at over 6,000 feet, and my blood has become accustomed.

Chacaltaya is the world's highest ski resort, but I wanted to go there, not to ski, but to photograph the surrounding peaks, snowcapped, black towards the foothills at this dry season of the year, and the strange-colored lakes, with their mineral content, which lie among the mountains.

"All right, you can stay in the car, take pictures through the window or, if you do get out, lean against it. Of course we'll bring along oxygen in case you need it.

The next day was still another of those clear days when the air seemed filtered, the clouds alive, the sun almost the royal divine Inti of the Incas. We started early to get there before the light was too intense. "Where's the oxygen?" I asked, as we rose into the stratosphere.

The guide patted my hand. "We forgot it." *Ni modo,* as they say in Mexico on such occasions, we did not need it, for the altitude, when we finally parked in a barren space beside a rough ski lodge, treated me to a different result. Exhilaration such as I had never felt. A desire, and I was sure an ability, to fly upwards to where the vultures circled, to join the clouds in their ballet across the sky. I mentioned the impulse to the guide. "Some people feel that way," he said. "It's like a half dozen Pisco sours."

"I'd like to stay here," I said obstinately. "Maybe get a job serving the coca tea, or at least washing the cups."

"You wouldn't like it after an hour or two," the guide said seriously. "The four boys who run this ski place can only work half time. They couldn't stand it otherwise."

How lucky I am! I recall reading Jose de Acosta's experience of mountain sickness as he described it: "When I came to the degrees, as they called them, which is the top of the mountain, I was suddenly seized with so mortal and strange a pang ... I was surprised with such pangs of straining and casting, as I thought to cast up my heart too, for having cast up meate, fleugme, and choller both yellow and greene, in the end I cast up blood. . ."

Hmmm.

"You could be right about staying up here," I said uneasily. "Guess we'd better start back."

***

Two American friends, Betty and Jake, arrived in La Paz and we went together to see Tiahuanacu, ruins of a civilization more ancient by far and less well known than that of the Incas.

We were escorted there by Victor Hugo, who was studying engineering, and acting as a guide on his time off. His father had offered to pay half his university expenses if he would earn the other half. His last name was Chavez or Sanchez, I forget which, but it was delightful to think of being escorted by a modern-day Victor Hugo with his shock of black hair, his acquiline Indian nose, his lithe young body of a soccer player (the La Paz team on Saturdays.)

"None of my blood is Inca," he told us proudly. "Partly I'm Spanish, of course, but the rest is Aymara. We never accepted the Incas. A million of us still speak Aymara, here around La Paz and Lake Titicaca."

On the way to the ruins we parked the car to take pictures of the cordillera, that vast chain of mountains, white-topped, stretching from one horizon to the other. Victor rattled off the names, but I gave up trying to jot them down. Besides, what difference, they are all huge peaks very like one another. Not at all, Victor said, they are not like one another. Each is different and each has different power.

"That one there" - he pointed to one of the jutting cones - "is my mountain, or rather I belong to it. It takes care of me, advises me. I go to the Street of the Witches and there one of those who knows consults dry coca leaves he has tossed onto the ground, and tells me what the mountain says."

Mount Huayna Potosí

"Wonderful! I'd like to have a mountain of my own too. I choose Huayna Potosí, the one near Chacaltaya, the one I photographed yesterday."

***

"You can't choose a mountain, Señora. It must choose you, through the diviners with the coca. You cannot consult them for serious answers. They would not tell your fortune, or advise you, you a foreigner."

The chauffeur called from the front seat, to be sure I understood. "No, no, Señora, nobody would tell your fortune."

I offered to hire Victor to go with me, talk the diviner into consulting whatever he consults, a llama fetus or a coca leaf, and give me the word. Victor laughed.

"I can never go with you," he said. "I am sorry."

The chauffeur chimed in. "He will never go with you, Señora, and I won't either. We are both sorry, but of course it is impossible."

"Victor, what did the mountain tell you last time you asked?" I spoke a little pettishly for I was disappointed.

"He gave me important advice."

"Which was?"

"That I should study harder at the University as I am not doing very well in math."

We passed a small chapel on top of a hill. "That's where people who die in road accidents go," Victor said. "They live forever there and their souls take care of us."

This college student tells me everything with conviction. Does he believe ti? Probably not, but perhaps just a little. In this thin mountain air, in this desolate brown *puna*, it would not be hard to believe. So a mountain is assigned to protect. The witch assigns it and then advises you on your behavior. Sometimes Indians still, when travelling from Lake Titicaca to La Paz, remove their knitted woolen hats and assume an attitude of prayer when they first come within sight of the cordillera, the range of sacred snowcapped peaks.

As we drove along, Victor Hugo kept us informed of interesting snatches of history and mythology. It was Sunday and plenty of campesinos had celebrated on Saturday night. A group of them reclined by the roadside in grotesque positions, like a battlefield after the fighting is over. Others had left the party, wherever it was, and wandered along the road uncertainly as though they were not sure of the location of home. Heaven, Victor told us as we passed the dregs of the party, is "a realm where the dead souls are forever plied with chicha but do not become drunk."

We met some llamas and he told us the story of a llama who began to pray and thus converted his master to the Christian faith. "Just a story, or course." He laughed. "I've lived here all my life and never yet seen a llama praying, but perhaps they do it at night."

There have been efforts by some researchers, he told us, to prove that Aymara was the original language of mankind. Of course *that* could be true. The name Tiahuanacu was originally in Aymara *Paypical,* which means "stone in the middle," the middle of the world, from which men set forth to repopulate the whole earth after the deluge. Strange how similar legends can be in different, unconnected parts of the world. Down in Cuzco it was once claimed that the original garden of Eden lay along the river at Urubambo.

"You can go to the lake," Victor told us, "and if you get tired of fishing for trout you can dive or dredge for treasure. The lake is full of gold and silver objects thrown there by the Indians at the time of the Spanish conquest, when the Inca Atahuallpa sent for his ransom. All sorts of riches were on their way to Cajamarca to buy the life of the sacred emperor. They came by bearer from every part of the kingdom, from north and south, east and west. When it was learned by *chasqui* that Atahuallpa had been executed by the enemy no mroe treasure was carried to Cajamarca, you may be sure of that. Nobody was giving precious things to the Spaniards to melt down and send across the ocean. Instead the treasure was hidden in caves and rivers, and much of it was tossed into the lake. If you were lucky you might still find some." Victor shook his head, frowning. For a moment the Spanish blood was not evident — he looked all Aymara. "I care about the history of my people," he told us. "So did my father and my grandfather also."

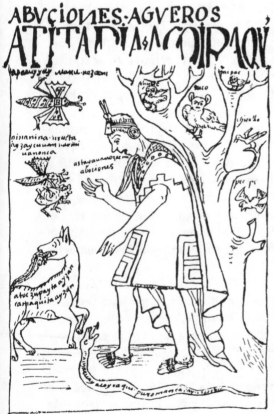

Superstitions

This was as near as Victor came to personal conversation. He gave mostly a parade of erudition, pieces of information he thought would be of interest to me.

He switched back and forth from fact to fancy. Wasn't this one place in the world where reality and unreality could freely mingle?

Waterfalls of melting snow beyond the city limits drive the generators for electricity. The cathedral took a hundred years to build. Indians think the stars are crumbs fallen from celestial banquets. Some diviners tell fortunes through the movements of spiders kept in jars. "It's not as dependable as the coca, and nobody will do that for your either, Señora, you a foreigner."

"Sorry, Señora, you can't have your fortune told that way," the driver, who had been listening intently, echoed from the front seat.

"Who said I wanted to have my fortune told by a spider? I'm only interested in mountains."

We passed two Indian women spinning with hand spindles, *pushcas,* as they walked. No Peruvian or Bolivian woman of the campo ever has idle hands. "Mama Ocllo, the goddess, always carried a *pushca,*" Victor told us. He went on to let us know that the llamas walking along by the road wore earrings of colored wool for a purpose.

"To prove ownership."

"Oh no, every llama knows his master and they know each other. The wool is put on them at the feast of San Juan to assure fertility."

The usual smallish dogs came out from the low chocolate-colored houses to bark at us as we passed; there was not much traffic going to Tiahuanacu. The houses, modest adobe dwellings, usually of three rooms, rose from the duncolored landscape like an afterthought of creation which, tired of the magnificence of mountains, had lowered itself to the simplicity of primitive human life. Of the three rooms, Victor said, one was the common living room, one the bedroom of the married couple, and the third for some leftover but not unwelcome family member, such as an unmarried sister. Attached to every house was a tiny replica, one room, done in the same architectural style if one can call it a style, of brown adobe, tiled roof, low entrance doorway. Does every family have a dwarf as member of the clan? No, these are meticulous doghouses, kennels given all possible dignity. The dog, while perhaps not on quite a social par with the llama, has his place in campesino life.

"Everybody has a dog."

"Everybody. To protect and to help with the sheep and to be part of the family."

We are approaching Tiahuanacu. "Our ruins are more impressive than Machu Picchu," Victor tells us. "Those Peruvians get their tourists by propaganda, publicity. That's how. Our Bolivian ruins are better. We have more to offer but not many people come."

True the ruins have much of interest to offer. However, a great deal of it is below ground for only part has been excavated, and from that part huge statues have been transported to special sites in downtown La Paz. The place is impressive still, especially the gateways of the sun, too monumental to move, but unlike Machu Picchu the ruins are almost deserted, with only one tour group of young Italians following the paths with us. Much of Machu Picchu's fame is dependent on its amazing geographical location, the mountain chasms, the river, the clouds reinforcing the drama of the scene. Tiahuanacu has none of this, situated as it is in a field between LaPaz and the lake.

Jake and Betty and I stroll through the excavated portions, conscious that beneath our feet still lies a buried city, sometime to be explored. The ruins are believed to date from 800 A.D., long before Manco Capac left Titicaca with his golden staff to found Cuzco. The Aymaras were first conquered by the Incas about 1450, resisting fiercely until they were finally subdued in 1485.

The Tiahuanacu culture is mysterious, antedating the Aymaras by centuries. It was long gone when the Spaniards arrived and there were no chroniclers to tell us about it. It may have been political in nature, an empire ruling a great part of the Andes in the time before the Incas, or perhaps it was religious, its influence extending from Ecuador to Chile. Like other ruined evidences of civilizations past it endured for centuries to be then abandoned for unknown reasons.

Here the altiplano, desolate, enormous, colored from tan through ochre to dull copper and rich brown, stretches far away. And here at Tiahuanacu not even the name of a mighty ruler is remembered. When the conquistadors arrived the Aymaras passed on only the legend that the buildings had been created in a single day. Even in the last century some explorers believed this to be the lost Atlantis, and the starting point of civilization.

At Tiahuanacu, as at Sacsahuaman and Machu Picchu, are incredible, enormous boulders, weighing tons, carefully fitted together, transported how? Every century has had its pet solution to this mystery. It was once thought to have been done by magic, with the devil working on it. Later it was suggested that an early race of giants moved mountains with ease. Maybe the rocks were melted, then hardened again in their places — but how? What about using water to turn wood into stone? In the nineteenth century it was imagined that the Incas had a special herb for making rock soft and malleable — but what herb? Right now the modern, up-to-the-minute notion is like the explanation for the mighty Nazca lines — extraterrestrial beings.

***

The ruins seen and photographed and those unseen imagined, we proceeded to the border of Peru at the Desaguadero River, for Jake and Betty were returning to Peru to visit other places. The countryside, as we passed along the shores of the lake, took on an intimacy quite alien to the puno from which we had just come. Titicaca was its usual vivid blue, the shores decorated with verdant totora reeds in clusters here and there, reed boats moving slowly among them. Colors of green, colors of blue, rich undreamed-of shades of brown. This was landscape where not a photographer but a watercolor artist was needed.

At Desaguadero we met the border again and the paved Peruvian highway again, but I was returning to La Paz to go on tomorrow to Sucre and I left my friends here — a slow parting since their Peruvian taxi had not arrived.

We waited, sitting on the international bridge, an ordinary looking bridge over an ordinary looking small river, with a history hundreds of years old, older than the rule of the Incas. The river is about one hundred feet wide and the bridge was constructed on balsa-reed pontoons with a road of rushes laid on top. Ropes fastened it to pillars on each side of the river. The balsas, becoming water-logged, had to be renewed every two years. The conqueror Francisco Pizarro took possession of the bridge, which was important for commerce and defense. It was constructed in its original primitive way, with pontoons replaced as needed, until 1867 when more modern technology took over.

We sat on the cement wall beside the bridge and ate our box lunches, besieged by dogs and children. We divided with the children, threw residue to the dogs. Hard to tell which leaped more eagerly for the treat. The dogs were pushy, the children polite. Two of the boys ran off home with sandwiches and apples, perhaps to share with the family.

Silver alpaca   discovered on the Island of Titicaca

In countries this poor it seems an insult to eat in front of the hungry, but none of the children looked undernourished. They probably hung around the bridge all day, where everyone must stop for immigration and customs, to make a meager living out of whatever turned up.

Finally the Peruvian driver turned up. "Just a little late, "he announced, checking his watch which said 12:30 instead of the promised 11:00.

Victor Hugo and the Bolivian driver awaited me, after I said goodbye to my friends, for the return trip to La Paz.

"Those Peruvians," the driver remarked, as I got in, "They're always late."

***

Victor decided to go with me to the airport to put me on my plane for Sucre. If Peruvian air traffic is unpredictable, Bolivian may be more so. Victor insisted on waiting in the airport lounge until the plane to Sucre not only landed, but was ready to board.

"Why don't you go home and study for your math exam?" I suggested.

"The plane may not go. Often they don't, and you have given up your hotel."

"But the plane's right there. I can see them fueling up. There's a line at the boarding gate."

"In Bolivia no one knows until it happens. However, things are not so bad here, even if we can't keep up with your American efficiency. I suppose I'd better go back and study."

I hadn't mentioned my efficiency, personal or national, but it is always on the minds of those who meet me in South America. They can't believe that I'd just as soon sit on a bench in the airport for a while and watch the world around me. Victor shrugged his shoulders and prepared to leave.

"Señora," he said earnestly. "I wish you luck. I hope you like our country. Anyway, as we say in our carnival song, we may have our failings and our problems, but, *A pesar de todo*, in spite of everything,

> *Hoy y manana*
> *Viva la nacion Boliviana!"*

He shook my hand and ambled off to the exit.

A church seen through arches—Sucre

BOLIVIA
A City of Bloood and Silver

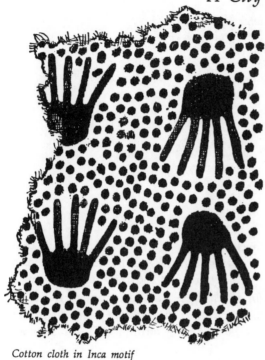

Cotton cloth in Inca motif

•*Sucre*
•*Tarabuco*
•*Potosí*

'In the
interminable
travels which the
white man forces
you to march,
chew the leaves.
The road will be
short and easy.
In the mines, where you will
be slaves, the juice of these leaves
will give you the illusion of happiness.

'But when the white man uses the
juice of this plant it will become an evil
vice for him. While for you, the Indian,
it is a spiritual sustenance, for him
it will cause madness.'

Beautiful princess
Your brother
Has broken
Your vase.
And that is why
It thunders, why lightning flashes
And thunderbolts roll.
But you, a princess,
Mistress of the rain,
You will give us water,
And, at other times,
Your hand will scatter hail,
Or snow.
Pachacamac,
Creator of the world,
And our god Virachocha
Have given you a soul
And a body
For this sole purpose.

The princess's vase had broken right over my head that afternoon in Sucre. The Incas and Aymaras had poems and prayers to invoke the rains, but what did they have to stop a downpour? I couldn't think of anything as I stood on one of the city's main streets with water sloshing around my ankles, water dripping from my hair, my ears, my nose, water penetrating the false resistance of my parka.

The street was lined with impressive centuries-old white houses, reserved, remote, distanced from me not only in the past but in the present. This could be an abandoned city, a group of architectural ruins. The sidewalk, only a few mintues ago full of pedestrians, was suddenly empty. A lone mule tied to a light pole at the corner pawed the muddy ground and shook his head. Water sprayed from his long ears.

Of course no sensible person would be abroad in this weather, not after reading the message of the rain clouds. I had not understood the messages, since I had been lulled to security by perpetual blue skies. Now I was not only drenched but lost. My hotel, an old mansion revived as a bed-and-breakdfast inn, was down one of these broad streets, but which one? Also, what was the name of the inn? I thought to return to the main plaza, but couldn't find that either. No map to consult; the tourist bureau had been out of them.

Entrances to Sucre cathedral

A clap of thunder, a flash of lightning. The deluge intensified.

I tried a turn to the left. It seemed familiar, and I realized I had been on it five minutes before. I stopped long enough to wipe the water from my eyes. Take it easy, slosh a few more blocks, I'd be bound to arrive. Lowering my head against a rising wind, I tried another turn to the left and came unexpectedly to the foot of a large cross set at an intersection. Familiar. No problem now. The storm, seeing me oriented, rapidly rolled away into the mountains. A watery sun came out.

I walked a few steps to the right, wading confidently, climbed a short flight of stairs, pushed open monumental doors, and stood in the small lobby of the Hostal Cruz de Popayán. The girl at the desk greeted me with enthusiasm.

"You've been wandering in the rain," she informed me. "Señora, you're wet!"

I changed my clothes and set out again, with the relentless blue sky once more above me, to explore the city.

As soon as I arrived in Sucre I realized that it was entirely different from La Paz; not only in its small size, but in its nostalgic feeling of great times gone by. It looked backward to when it was the home of rich mine owners, the unchallenged center of the district of Charcas and the territory of Upper Peru.

Sucre is still the actual capital of Bolivia, although big, bustling, breathless La Paz is the de facto center. Sucre has gradually lost all of its government centers except the supreme court, which it holds onto jealously. So it's still the capital, right? Memories of former importance appear in the building surrounding the main plaza: the Legislative Palace, the Palace of Justice, the Government Building. Sucre is a pleasant, lazy city where night life stops early and it's hard to find a decent restaurant.

Wandering into a park, I discovered the Paris my friend in La Paz had mentioned. Not content with stately palaces, a university, elegant promenades, Sucre indeed offers copies of French structures: a toy version of the Arc de Triomphe, a miniature Rue de la Paix, an Eiffel Tower where children climb as on a jungle gym. French is a popular major at the University and the Alliance Francaise keeps citizens alerted to European culture. Looking for a good meal, I was directed to the restaurant at the Alliance, for a quiche and wine. An optimistic recommendation: what I found, as the night's specialty, was a hamburger and beer.

The several small Andean cities which I have visited — Sucre, Cuenca, Arequipa — have much in common. Everyone reads the papers, watches TV, and worries about world events, but outside problems seem a bit removed, while history remains close at hand and cherished. Until airplane travel burgeoned people here were isolated, living more in memory than in current events. An hour's journey now was then a matter of a day or two. Whether the sudden haul into the stress of modern city life is good who can say? Sucre appears unruffled. Says one of my guidebooks, "Long isolation has helped it to preserve its courtly charm."

Such provincial cities as Sucre are interesting to visit, not only for their own sake, but because there are always simpler villages within an easy drive. Tarabuco, a couple of hours by car or bus from Sucre, is noted for its Sunday market, said by some market aficionados to be the best in South America. I didn't find it outstanding but then, after years of living in Mexico, I am market-hardened. Its woolen goods are exceptionally fine, but I remember chiefly the range of vivid colors of the items set out upon the ground for sale, at total contrast with the khaki-colored hills around: the red, orange and yellow of fruits and vegetables, the brilliant green of shiny coca leaves overflowing their huge hampers.

Tarabuco is dominated by the usual country church, and in the main square a statue, laughably bad, shows an Indian drinking something or other, or possibly blowing a horn. Many Tarabucans still wear the famous local hats, surely in some sort of mockery, for they are an imitation of helmets worn by the Spaniards during the conquest, when Indians of this area put up a particularly savage resistance. The statue wears such a helmet, and his story still gives residents a good laugh.

The Tarabucans, holding out against the men from Castile, those centuries ago were far outnumbered. Word came that they would be attacked and slaughtered by a huge enemy force.

There was nothing to do but to flee to the hills, leaving the women and children to mind the village. The Spaniards attacked, were furious at finding no warriors to kill, and slaughtered all the families. In revenge the Tarabucans ambushed the Spanish leader and, as my informant explained with a pleasant smile, "bit out his heart, eating it while he still lived." No doubt the statue of the chieftain commemorates the deed, as he quaffs a beaker of blood.

Guidebooks give the year 1538 as the date when the Spanish founded Sucre, but it had been an Indian city long before that. Its past existed in layers, the Inca layer dating from 1200 AD when Inca Roca, ruler of Cuzco, subdued the Charcas Indians, making Chuquisaka, as it was then called, the capital of the great district of Charcas in the Empire of Tahuantinsuyo. Here a privileged Inca city rose between the two hills of Churuquilla and Sicasica. According to tradition one was a hill of gold and the other of silver. It was a city of gardens and green fields whose inhabitants, from peasant to nobles, worked together at agriculture, without distinction of age or sex, singing as they worked. They found peace and contentment in the richness of the fields, where they raised fine corn under the splendor of the upland sky.

Following is a story told by the Bolivian author, Antonio Paredes-Candia, who has preserved his country's folklore in a series of books.

Life at Chuquisaka was proceeding in an idyllic fashion until one day word came by *chasqui* runner, telling of white men who grew hair on their faces, gave out flashes of lightning, and charged about on wild animals. They had taken the great Inca, Atahuallpa, prisoner in Cajamarca, a city far to the north. Only an enormous ranson could buy his freedom. There was much gold and silver stored in secret caves outside Chuquisaka. Three weeks went by during which this treasure was brought from all over the province of Charcas and piled up in the chief's mansion. It would be taken to the place where strangers held the royal Sun against his will. The Tarabuco tribe organized an expedition to transport the ransom, carrying it twenty-five leagues, then passing it on to another band, and so on until finally, reaching its destination hundreds of leagues to the north, it would buy their ruler's freedom.

The story is still told this way: On a dry hot day in September, 1533, Tango-Tanga, the head man of Tarabuco, led a group of Indians with heavy loads of treasure across the pass outside Chuquisaka, heading towards the Abra del Sol between the gold and silver mountains. The party was only a league short of rendezvous with the next group of bearers when a runner met them. Panting with exhaustion he raised his hand; it was a moment before he could speak. Then he told them: "The great Inca, Atahuallpa, has been killed. The white men have murdered him. Gold and silver will not help. Carry your loads back again."

While his group of bearers waited, Tanga-Tanga frowning, considered the news. Finally, he spoke: "Listen. We can no longer live when our leader, the Sun, has been foully killed. We will go to the cave in the mountain; that will be our burial place."

The men, used to commands, said nothing. They turned and trudged back between the gold and silver mountains. Finally they reached a cave where Tanga-Tanga told them to halt. The entrance was blocked by a huge boulder.

"Move it," Tanga-Tanga ordered. The bearers did so, after an hour's struggle. Then they followed their chief into the deep cave, which was empty and black as night.

"Close the entrance," Tanga-Tango said. His followers hardly hesitated. They dragged and rolled the giant boulder back until it blocked the entrance. No one spoke a word, and they were silently entombed within, forever.

That is the Indian version of history. The Spaniards never found the treasure cave. When they arrived at the Inca city, led by Don Francisco Pizarro, to found the Villa de la Plata y de los Caballeros (now Sucre), the natives abandoned their idyllic life and fled to the mountains where they hid in the inpenetrable forest. It was only after a good many years, when La Plata had developed into a Spanish metropolis, that the Indians of Chuquisaca returned and learned to live there again.

La Plata prospered. People in this healthy climate were said to live until a great age, 120 ... even 130 years. It became a city of residence of grandees and nouveaux riches, to escape the rugged frontier life of the Potosí minefields. Here they built themselves the graceful homes among which I had been lost, centuries later, in the rain.

***

Potosí was an unlikely city: at one time the biggest metropolis in the western hemisphere, set in the barren reaches of the altiplano at an elevation of more than 13,000 feet. It lived, grew, and prospered from the enormous riches of silver found in the conelike hill, the Cerro Rico.

Life in the mines

The Jesuit chronicler, José de Acosta, writing in 1590, told of the Indians' discovery of the Potosí mines before the arrival of the Spanish conquistadors.

"An Indian called Guanca, going one day to hunt for venison ... beganne to run up against the rocke, which at that time was covered ... with certaine trees ... He was forced to lay hold upon a branch, which issued from a veine of a silver mine ... perceiving the hole or foot there of mettall the which he knew to be very good."

However, the word Potosí means "noise" in Quechua, and to the Incas it was a forbidden place. There had been a rumble from within it, a command from God to leave the treasure alone for those who would come later. So the Cerro Rico, the hill of riches, waited until 1545 when Juan de Villareal y Santadia rediscovered it. A year later the city was established, the silver rush was on.

By 1573 Potosí had a population of 120,000, equal to that of London. By the end of the century it had 594 streets, 16,000 houses. This made it the first city of the Americas and one of the most important in the world. By 1650 its 160,000 inhabitants far outnumbered those of Buenos Aires and Lima with 4,000 apiece, and even Mexico City with its 30,000.

During those times it developed the violent, romantic, fascinating aspect of all bonanza cities, outclassing every one of them for stories of fierce duels, love and hate, infidelity, treachery, murder, mayhem ... stories often leading belatedly to moralistic endings.

The Incas, though they did not work Potosí before the Spaniards came, had other rich mines from which they extracted precious metals. As a benevolent dictator the Inca took care of his miners. The work was managed carefully, a laborer putting in only four months of work per year, in the warm season. He had his relatives close by. Indeed no one was assigned to the mines unless he was married and could bring along his family to look after his food and drink. Since he could not cultivate the fields back home others were appointed to plant crops for him at the proper season, and if the worker became sick he went home at once. Miners never died from overwork.

Under the Spaniards it was different. The mines could not be operated without forced labor, Indian labor, which necessitated drafting natives for the job from as far away as Argentina and northern Peru. From one area alone 7,000 workmen and 40,000 animals (mostly llamas) journeyed for three months every year to labor in the desolate altiplano.

On every shift some 4,500 Indians climbed down rickety rawhide ladders to the bottom of a 750 foot shaft. A worker was required to haul a hundred pounds of ore at a time on his back up the ladder. In the beginning work shifts were eight hours long, but there were not enough Indians to fill the demand for riches. The work period increased to six days without a break, and increasing numbers of Indians were brought in to replace those who had died. After six days a leader was dispatched to bring to the surface those Indians who had survived, marching them in a candlelight procession down the Hill of Riches.

The laborers worked under the influence of coca, chewing the leaf continuously, even rubbing their picks with it in the hope it would give greater strength to their tools. In Inca times coca chewing had been reserved for the upper classes; now it was the sedative of the slave. The coca plant became the leading cash crop of the Spanish Viceroyalty.

A Spanish chronicler wrote: "In the rich entrails of this admirable mountain resound the blows of the picks, the voices and groans of the workers, the shouts of the overseers ... Some do not know the openings underfoot, and falling into wells and lagoons of great depth, are drowned, while others are buried under falling rocks. You will see them, laden with metal, climb up ropes and descend great depths by thin stocks, and through missing their footholds fall to their deaths. You will see them crawling on all fours like beasts with a load on their backs, or dragging themselves along on their stomachs like worms."

The adventurers, entrepreneurs and fortune seekers, who filled the upper strata of society, came from all over the world. They had nothing in common with the Indian labor force. The Indians squatted in hovels, the white men built fine houses for themselves — if they struck it rich, that is. If not, they might retreat across the desolate plain, poverty-stricken and hungry.

Potosí town was known as a "city of blood and silver" where personal feuds were so common that the place seemed to be always in civil war. Ladies, resplendent in silks from the Orient and pearls from Venezuela, went to the city's main square as to a bull fight. There were eight fencing schools to teach self-protection, and a choice of 36 gaming houses where feuds might start. Hostility could also spring from rivalry between mine owners. Licenses were issued for thousands of mines, many of which were closed by avalanches of debris cascading down from mines higher up the Silver Hill.

Violence in the city

The mint, the Casa de Moneda,

which is today a museum, covered two city blocks and turned out during Colonial times a total of some two billion ounces of silver, in reales, half-reales, pieces of eight.

A complicated process changed the ore into precious metal. First it was beaten on anvils, then the powder passed through a fine sieve to be spread on the ground in a smooth area. Much water was poured through it, and it was then spread with quicksilver and iron, the mass stirred at intervals for a fortnight, wetting it daily with water. It was then milled to take out the earth and water, put in a crucible to remove the quicksilver, and finally delivered to the mint for assay.

The silver had still to be transported from Potosí to Spain half way around the world. It went by mule train to Arica on the Pacific, thence by small ship to Lima. From there it journeyed northward in two great galleons accompanied by various small merchant vessels, the whole convoy preceded by little pinnaces sailing eight or ten leagues ahead to "make discoveries," for there were pirates, especially Englishmen, eager to get their hands on the cargo.

The galleons could have reached Panama in a couple of weeks, but they never took much less than a month because the captains were entrepreneurs, making a tidy income selling playing cards to passengers who were eager to gamble their wealth of silver. It was remarked of such a captain: "He received for each pack 10 patacoons ... and the quantity sold was plentiful, for play went on continuously, and it rarely happened that there were any on board who were not interested in gambling."

priest & governor gambling

When the galleons reached Panama, with much of the wealth no doubt redistributed, the silver bullion went over the isthmus by mule back to Portobello on the Atlantic, where another fleet of galleons set sail for Havana, thence to Cadiz. These treks continued for hundreds of years, the last treasure fleet sailing in 1796.

***

Meanwhile, back in Potosí ... "The people here live on another level from the rest of the world, and the getting and spending of money is a fever that burns and possesses the whole population ...They always go in cloth of gold and silver, or in scarlet silk ... In general they eat and cook off silver plate."

"Wives are kept very close to a degree beyond what they are in Spain — they never go abroad unless to be together to mass or to make some visit, or to some public feast, and that but rarely."

There were no less than sixty churches in Potosí, whether for devout wives or repentant sinners. And there were an abundant number of houses of prostitution.

If blood flowed in the central plaza on Potosí, as men mowed each other down in duels, fiestas were equally spectacular. One, which was described in detail by several foreign visitors, was that celebrating the birth of the Prince of Spain in 1658. For this event the streets were paved with blocks of silver. The rejoicing for the birth of the Infante, so many thousands of miles away, went on for a fortnight with parades and balls, masquerades and comedies. The most extravagant procession approached the plaza from the outskirts of the city, while ladies at windows and on balconies tossed down perfumed water and dry sweetmeats. The parade included the replica of a ship of a hundred tons, her sails billowing in the following wind as she was towed through the streets. As soon as she arrived at the plaza she saluted the crowd by the discharge of all her cannon.

Other features of the procession were a mock castle where Cromwell was supposed to be immured, a fleet of smaller ships, and such novelties as horses trained to dance. Gold and silver was thrown among the crowd. There were fireworks, which eventually burned up the ship, the small boats and the castle, presumably with Cromwell in it.

Well, of course I had to visit the city where such events had occurred even though it was now pretty well emptied. The silver bonanza was followed by the reign of tin, from which fortunes were made, but now, with the price of tin bottomed-out on the world market, most of the mines were closed either because of failures or of workers strikes.

Potosí is several hours from Sucre by train. That kind of journey offers no good photo opportunities, as I had learned from previous encounters with dirty train windows, vibration on the uneven track which jiggled my camera, and the eagerness of the motorman to speed past the most interesting scenery. Once in Potosí I'd have to spend the night, or two nights if I wanted to see anything much, and then return again by train.

I decided to hire a car and driver-guide, especially after I met Don Miguel. He was not your usual chauffeur: everyone used the courtesy term "Don" when speaking to him, and he was recognized as an authority on the past. He was an affable man of fifty or so.

"We can get there and have a good day's sightseeing if we leave early," he told me. "Say four in the morning."

"All right," I said, "I'll be ready, but where can we get coffee at that hour?"

The women in the travel agency where I had met Don Miguel offered to put up a vacuum of coffee and make ham sandwiches the night before. There was much leisurely discussion of how much cream? sugar? mustard on the ham? white or dark rolls?

"You will like this trip," Altagracia told me. She doubled her job as agency manager with that of curator of one of the museums and had been bringing me choice books to read every evening. "You will like it especially because I am sure Don Miguel will tell you stories. He knows more than anyone in Sucre about the history and legends of the province."

Don Miguel smiled. "I've made it my life's work. Driving a car is not really a life's work, you know."

I was ready at four next morning, dressed in a double layer of slacks, three sweaters and a wool cap, for the altiplano is cold at night even in the spring months which, since it was October, was the present season. Don Miguel turned up as the cathedral clock boomed the hour.

We set out through deserted streets. As we left town a few campesinos were coming in with produce on muleback, and a night bus passed us, its brakes screeching on the curves.

"Let's have the coffee right now, Don Miguel," I suggested. "It will take the chill off."

"No coffee. They were going to bring it to my house but no one came. You can never trust these girls in offices." He lit a cigarette. "There's a place to have coffee a couple of hours from here, and we'll be in Potosí by ten o'clock in time for our almuerzo."

"If we can't have coffee, then tell me a story," I said. "Tell me about the old times."

***

"*Naupa pacha*", he began. "That's the way the Incas started their tales ... Once upon a time. First a story of this very province of Charcas.

"It was in this province at a wild place called Llama Chaki, the Llama's Foot, the part of the altiplano where caves in the mountains are filled with stalagmites and stalactites. That's where Linda Sirena, the sorceress, lived on the Enchanted Mountain. She wore an extra large white tunic and the sound of her beautiful voice, clear as water falling, was always an omen of disaster. Inca treasurers were buried in a deep cave there, as we know they are in many parts of this land. They were guarded by a *chullpa*, one of our ancient burial tombs, and by a condor named Mallku, who was a magician as well as a bird. His crest was carmine, his feathers the color of ashes. Mallku's job was to weep tears of blood if any human came near; then, with a violent flap of his ash-gray wing he would knock the intruder into the abyss.

"In Llama Chaki lived also the terrible Auki and the Indian woodman, Jaturro, with his nasty deformed head. Jaturro sold wood every morning in nearby Torotoro — it's over that way, still too dark for you to see it—and bought coca leaves. He wore tattered clothes and was shy like a ferret. After trading his wood for coca he would disappear in the afternoon, climbing into the heights of the mountains playing his melancholy flute and singing old Inca songs.

"Then one day he unexpectedly turned up well dressed, looking rich. 'He must be a thief,' the people in Torotoro said immediately. He was arrested, with even his indispensable coca placed beyond reach. Under torture he confessed that he got his money from Auki at the cave of the *chullpa*, exchanging coca for it.

"The people of Torotoro, eager to share in such wealth, escorted Jaturro to Llama Chaki where they easily captured the infamous Auki, netting him with a lasso as he came out of the cave for his basket of coca. They tied him in a sack and returned triumphant to Torotoro. 'We'll lock you up until you tell us where the treasure is,' the chief said.

"Auki really was a horrible looking fellow, less than a meter tall, with a long beard, double rows of teeth like a cayman, and the nails of a black bear. He gobbled coca and answered no questions. They shut him up for the night in the Peña house — the Peña descendants still live there and tell about it. A ferocious dog kept guard ready to bark at the slightest movement. However, in the morning when a huge crowd gathered to inspect the monster, he had vanished. A committee was formed to find the *chullpa* cave and bring back the treasure. They forced Jaturro to lead them there again.

"When they arrived at the cave it was pitch black night and they were more than a little nervous. There was no moon, the stars gave no light, a melancholy wind howled through the clefts in the rock. Nobody wanted to be first to enter the cave, so they all camped outside.

"Two days later the townsfolk, their families and friends, came looking for them, and found them all hanged to Auki's rock except for Jaturro who had hurled himself into the abyss. Ever since then, the grandmothers of Torotoro will tell you, on dark nights a black shadow wanders in those regions and heartrending cries issue from *chullpa* ravine. The condor still takes his majestic flight in the heavens, looking down on the enchanted mountain which forever keeps its counsel, and the Siren, in her big white tunic, sings."

***

The sun had risen now and we pulled up at a small cafe where workmen and farmers were eating buns and drinking hot black coffee.

"That was a good story, wasn't it?" Don Miguel remarked, as he opened the restaurant door in a courtly manner for me to go in. He adjusted his steel-rimmed glasses, stroked his moustache.

"Yes it was," I said. "What do you think about that kind of story, Don Miguel? Do you think it was entirely made up, or that it was based on some event; after all there must be a lot of treasure around here still, if we only knew where to find it. The Incas surely hid what they could when the conquerors came, and some of it must never have been reclaimed."

Don Miguel smiled, sipped his coffee, shook his head, "Well, it's a good story," he said.

After coffee we went out to the car again and the world now seemed real. Before, while Don Miguel was storytelling, and the landscape was dark except for our headlights on the gravel road, we had been passing through a dream world, a vast expanse of darkness, perhaps in a time before creation, when the whole universe waited for a bang or a burst of light.

The burst of light had come now all right, and also the burst of sounds as two men approached, practicing on their trumpets as they walked. A contest of some sort, rehearsal for a celebration, an assuagement of the soul after a night of chicha drinking? Whatever it concerned, it must be a contest for the musician who could hit the most wrong notes.

We got into the car. "I have lots more to tell you if you care to hear it," Don Miguel said, turning on the engine. He looked at me hopefully. I nodded. "That's good. At least my grandchildren like it. I tell them stories which must be exciting. They fall asleep right away."

"I won't fall asleep," I said, "at least, not right away. I think I can make it to Potosí."

"My next story is about Potosí itself." Don Miguel slowed down for a curve. We had lingered over coffee and the sun, the great Inti, was well up above the horizon. We left the town and the bare land stretched away on either side, that dun color which I associated with the altiplano. Even though the first rain had fallen it was still the dry season. Far away on the right I could see small human figures and a tractor.

"It looks like a big farm," I said.

"Yes. They have cooperative farms here. Most of our Bolivians in the country are terribly poor, but when they band together like this they prosper. There's a good market for potatoes, wheat and barley. The single farmers, though, can never do more than scratch a living with their digging sticks and hoes, which are the same as in Inca days.

"We call this highway for President John F. Kennedy," he went on. "It was through aid from your country that we began cultivating this one in a modern fashion. This road, for instance, we owe to you and it is fine." Indeed it was smoother than most Bolivian highways.

"We have our problems," Don Miguel said, "but we have our good times too." (I never met a Bolivian who would admit to being desperate in the desperate condition of his country.) He started to hum, then sang a few lines. I caught only the familiar refrain, which I had heard from Victor in La Paz.

> "A pesar de todo
> Hoy y mañana.
> Viva la nacion Boliviana."

"Well, this story, since it's about Potosí, will be quite Spanish. Nothing Inca in it at all. The Spaniards were busy in those days working the Indians to death in the mines. Later there were laws to protect them. The city was ruled by a governor who, however, spent his time in La Plata, our Sucre, traveling by horseback over much the same route we are driving on this Kennedy highway.

"Everybody came to Potosí with high hopes. Everybody was a caballero, a gentleman, even if he was starving to death, and a man who yesterday hadn't even a shirt, tomorrow might have 50,000 pesos, rich as a great lord. Those who made it did live like lords. They used to say about one such: 'The Pope in Rome, the King in Spain and Domingo Beltran in Potosí.' Then there was the Spaniard who lived on the town of Porco and worked in Potosí. His wife sent him every day a dinner she had cooked in Porco and it arrived in Potosí, seven leagues away, still hot. I wonder how she did it?"

There was a straight stretch of highway ahead, and at the end of it I thought I could glimpse a hill — the silver mine, of Cerro Rico? "You were going to tell me another story," I said. "Let's hear it before we get there."

"You like my stories? Good. I hope you don't mind if there's lots of blood. There were two Spanish ladies in Potosí who knew each other, and of course one of them was good, one wicked. Otherwise how could we have a story? Claudia, the villainess, was beautiful, the queen of the fiestas. She only played with love until one day she met a handsome general who spurned her advances for he loved only his wife. Naturally *he* was the man she must have, and of course his wife, Doña Leonor Fernandez de Cordoba, was an angel on earth who never did or even thought anything wrong in her life."

"A prig?" I said in English.

"Probably. I don't know that word, but your language is a mystery, isn't it? She certainly was *mojigata*. However, in these stories you have to love the heroine, it's a rule. That's what I tell Berto, my grandson.

"Claudia spread doubts about Doña Leonor's virtue, and people gossiped, for her husband was away on business a great deal, and in a town like Potosí that was simply calling for trouble. Leonor's virtue was untarnished, however. Nobody could accuse her of anything. So Claudia sent an anonymous message to Leonor's husband who was in Cuzco. An Indian runner arrived on foot at Cuzco, the best and greatest city the earth has ever seen, and delivered the message which was full of lies. The husband, when he read the note, had sneaking doubts, as who wouldn't in faraway Cuzco with his wife in licentious Potosí, a wife as beautiful as his Leonor. He consulted an old Priest in the Sun.

"They met and stood together on a hill near the Royal City. When the moon was high above them they called on the shades of the dead as they sacrificed a llama and studied its entrails."

"Great Pachacamac," the Indian cried. "The red stain from the llama signifies blood!" Indeed it did since the llama had bled to death. Leonor's husband, alarmed by the prophecy, hurried back to Potosí. He wrote to Claudia, his wife's good friend, to ask what she made of the matter.

"Claudia got busy. She bribed Leonor's maid to sneak a man into the salon at night so that Leonor's husband saw him leaving. Furious, he rushed in to the room and killed his wife with blows of his sword. Soon Leonor was dead and the salon was full of blood, which must have been what the Indian in Cuzco foretold.

"It wasn't long after the murder that Leonor's husband realized he had been wrong, his wife was blameless. He ran away from Potosí and the house was abandoned. They say Doña Leonor appears sometimes, late at night, in her salon, a red ghost shivering in a rain of blood. As for Claudia, and we do of course have to dispose of her... two of her beaus killed her at the gaming table."

***

Scattered houses appeared, the road climbed upward. "We're coming to the city soon," Don Miguel said, "and I'm ready for *almuerzo*, it's past ten o'clock. I'll take you to a restaurant which belongs to my uncle who puts on a really tasty lunch. Then we'll look around, you can take pictures, and I'll tell you everything that went on in the old days; although there won't be time to tell you half of it, the place was so busy when the silver was here."

Don Miguel and I walked up to the second floor of the Casa Taurina to a good smell of chicken soup and fried fish.

***

After lunch Don Miguel went off to visit a friend while I took pictures here and there. Potosí is a hill town, Colonial in style, quiet now with only the memory of bawdy, violent boom days. In the main square the Potosínos pass at a leisurely walk, giving a curious glance to a visitor. There are tourists, of course, but no crowds of them, for the silver city will not fit into a three day tour of Bolivia. In the main

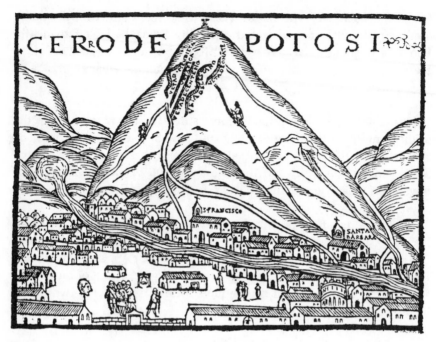

Potosí

square I heard voices that had to come from down under. Two young men with back packs approached. We exchanged greetings.

"From Australia?" I suggested.

"No, New Zealand. Are you here for long? We could have dinner together."

I explained that I was heading back to Sucre in the afternoon. I wondered, as I often have, why more Americans don't come to Bolivia, so much more accessible to them than to these distant travelers.

We chatted a moment, then I went on to the Casa de Moneda, the huge mint-museum which takes a couple of hours to explore. Don Miguel met me there to drive me up to the mines.

"Many of the mines are shut now," he explained, "because of strikes. The price of tin has fallen and the wages to match it. A man cannot feed his family. But I'll take you up to see the view, if nothing else."

Potosí town is at over 13,000 feet elevation. The mining area up on the Cerro de Plata, the Noisy mountain of riches, is even higher. I panted a little as we got out of the car to look around. Not much work going on. One young man came out of a dark tunnel and stood for his photograph. "Bad times," he said and trudged away down the hill.

We came back from the Cerro and I sat again for a while in the main square where the past was rudely present in my imagination. I thought of the legends I had read of souls in torment, the goblins and supernatural creatures. They belonged to Potosí, where passions flared and furious impulses led to violence. Why should the men of those days resist such impulses? Poor today, rich tomorrow, or the other way around. Why not live today, dead tomorrow? All those adventurers were gambling with their lives or they would not have set out from Central America, from North America, from Europe, from Argentina or Brazil, traveling over rugged, unfamiliar country, journeying for months by mule back, by river raft, on foot, to reach a legendary El Dorado in the middle of this mud-brown landscape.

Some of those fortune seekers must have lived a bit outside reality. That was natural. Not everyone who journeys through such hardships for dubious rewards remains fully in command of his senses, or perhaps he never was in command of them.

There was that legendary pilgrim of Potosí, whose story I had read, a wanderer who entered a house in the Calle de la Plata where gaming was going on. He was a stranger but the gamblers accepted his presence with no comment. People came and went in Potosí, and no one asked questions. Some were seen often, others quickly left forever carrying riches, or else the bitter memory of failure. This fellow was different: A bird, some kind of crow kept following him around. The gamblers offered the visitor a drink but when he raised the glass to his mouth the bird cawed and he set it down untasted. The man's eyes gleamed like fireflies. He came and went often to the house on Calle de la Plata, never talking, never joining the game. He would always enter with his bird — a crow? a raven? - accept a drink and set it down untasted when the crow cawed.

Finally the stranger made a last visit and left, explaining simply, "I am going to enjoy the presence of God." The gamblers said masses for the departed stranger, and eventually the true story was told: The crow was the spirit of the stranger's friend from whom he had stolen a jewel and whom he had then murdered — never again to rid himself of the raven-ghost and its cawing.

Potosí society, in the 16th century, believed that because of the many violent deaths in the city, the blood and the fighting, there were numberless souls suffering in purgatory. Their phantoms accounted for mysterious noises, rustling and groaning in many a town house.

Fiestas often turned into battles. For a while Potosí was the scene of war between two rival gangs, the Vicuñas and the Vascongado. It wasn't until 1624 that they reconciled. The legend was that Potosí people couldn't resist the smell of blood. One duel was even fought between two sisters and two brothers, which the sisters won.

These legends sound authentic: events which took place in the never-never land of a huge metropolis enjoying enormous wealth at the very edge of the world.

The city was built in two sections, the Indians in the gulleys, the Spaniards on the more desirable heights. The river of Caricari ran through Potosí, its waters overflowing in the rainy months from January to April. The Virrey del Peru, Don Francisco de Toledano, built a complicated hydraulic system, assigning forty Indians to care for it. Its overflow was called, in Quechua, the River of Content, but there must have been little content among the Indians, working themselves to death in the mines, nor among the foreigners, living dangerous lives which could lead to sudden death.

The Potosí Fair, started in 1625, was known as the richest in the world. Indians arrived from leagues away, with their llamas, coca, baskets of corn, blankets of ordinary alpaca wool or finest *chumpi*. There were mountains of imported goods, for the rich miners could afford anything, even to rugs from Cairo or Persia.

***

"Well," said Don Miguel, finding me wandering the back streets. "There's much to see here, Señora Celia. One could never tire of the memories, which of course one cannot see, or have you been seeing them perhaps? You look a little *distraida*. If we were staying the night you might speak to a ghost or hear a soul crying in purgatory. As it is, we'd better get started back to Sucre."

We left and on the way home Don Miguel finally did put me to sleep with his stories. After all, we made an early start before the paling of dawn. We drove back to Little Paris over the same road, Don Miguel keeping himself awake by story-telling, even though I heard only snatches . . . The mysteriously vanished cave where a dog perpetually barked, the lake where no one swam for often a swimmer might disappear, tales of banquets given in the old days, blow by blow accounts of bloody encounters.

"I guess you never run out of stories, do you, Don Miguel?" I woke for a moment to look at a black sky, a somber barren landscape with two or three lights glimmering low to the ground in mud houses along the way.

"Well, no" he agrees, "I don't but I guess there must be an end. I have enjoyed the privilege of telling you these things, Señora Celia, and you can put them in your book. Of course every word is true." He grinned. "You are going to write a book about us who live in Bolivia?"

"Perhaps."

"Don't forget to tell about the barking dog and the dueling sisters. Yes, and the bridge at Laja, but that I forgot to tell you."

I kept my eyes open with an effort. We should be approaching Sucre soon, and I thought with longing of my comfortable bed in the Hostal Cruz de Popayán.

"You had better let me hear one more story now. Otherwise, perpaps I will never hear it. Who knows if I will be back this way?"

"Who knows, Señora Celia. *Naupa pacha* ...Once upon a time ...I won't tell you about the bridge but about the coca, a plant which seems to interest you foreigners unduly. The Indians never processed it to make cocaine, but simply chewed the leaves so that they could endure the sufferings the invaders imposed on them."

Don Miguel was obviously *mestizo*, of mixed blood, with Spanish heritage predominant, but he sided emotionally with the indigenous oppressed. I later came across this same story in one of Paredes-Candia's books of legends. Don Miguel, however, had made it his own, pretending it happened to him.

"I have done a lot of traveling in the altiplano," he said, "in my younger days. That always meant camping out at night for there were no inns and, along with the Indians who were used to it, travelers like me lay down and wrapped themselves in blankets against the freezing night air. The Indians, who were in better shape because they had been chewing bitter coca all day, did not sleep either, but they relaxed, living the old times vicariously, the years before the coming of the conqueror. They have not forgotten although it is now hundreds of years since the conquest.

"They built a fire, gathering around it companionably, perhaps tossing in a bit of corn or red pepper, in case their ancestors might appear as sparks and complain of hunger. Here is a favorite Indian story, which I have heard more than once:

"It was shortly after the white conquerors had landed from the sea, coming under the guise of gods although they were imposters. They murdered Atahuallpa at Cajamarca, even though he paid undreamed-of ransom. That's the sort of men they were. They not only carried away our royal treasures, they profaned and demolished our sacred temples. They destroyed our cities so that we abandoned our fields and fled into the forests or the caves in the heights of the gray and holy mountains. We wept for the fate of our people, for our sons and brothers exiled or slaughtered. We have never forgotten that time, which had been foretold as *pachatikray*, the end of the world.

"The story teller paused a minute to toss another piece of llama dung onto the fire. He chewed his coca and swallowed with a grunt of satisfaction.

"The old sorcerer who had served the Inca on the Island of the Sun, in the great lake, fled before the invaders arrived, carrying with him the sacred treasure from the shrine. He hid it in a secret spot on the eastern shore of Lake Titicaca. He stayed there watching for Pizarro's men, and when one day he saw them coming he hurled the treasure, the gold and silver and precious jewels, into the deep lake. Of course he would not tell the Spaniards what he had done, but suffered torture in silence. When they grew tired of questioning and learning nothing, they left the old man in agony and went to make their own search for the treasure.

"That night the sorcerer dreamed that Inti, the Sun, appeared from behind the nearest mountain peak and said, "My son, your heroism in defending my sacred treasure deserves a reward. Ask whatever you wish from me."

"'Of course I want my people saved, the enemy destroyed. What else could I ask for?"

"Inti, the Sun, answered sadly, "That is something I cannot do, for their god is more powerful than mine. They have robbed me of my kindgom and I, just like you, am fleeing, seeking a refuge in the mystery of time. However, before I go I will give you something within my power. What do you want?"

'I have to think it over before deciding. I need the rest of my life to consider the matter.'

"'I can give you only one moon's time.' Thereupon the Sun disappeared among red clouds.

"'Some of our people endured the slavery the white men brought; others fled across the great lake in small totora reed boats. They hid on the east bank where they found the sorcerer near death. Remembering the Sun's promise, the old man decided to ask for something, anything, that would comfort his people. That night he made a last request of the Sun.

"'Great Inti, give us something for our pain."

"Suddenly a mysterious force lifted him from the shore of the lake, wafted him through the air, and set him gently down on a hilltop. Here, in contrast to the cold silent black night, a great light shone. Inti spoke.

"My son, you wish to leave your miserable brothers something to help them. Look around you. Do you see those bushes with oval green leaves? They are a miraculous cure for exhaustion, for the bitter days. Tell your brothers to pick the leaves, dry them and chew them. This will relieve the terrible pain of their souls."

"The old man returned to his hut just as dawn began to illuminate the earth and turn the water of the great lake to silver. 'My sons,' he told his companions, 'I am dying, but first I must tell you that the Sun, our God, has given us a gift: Climb the hill over there and find the plants with oval leaves. They will offer comforts to your spirits.

'In the interminable travels which the white man forces you to march, chew the leaves. The road will be short and easy. In the mines, where you will be slaves, the juice of these leaves will give you the illusion of happiness.'

'But when the white man uses the juice of this plant it will become an evil vice for him. While for you, the Indian, it is a spiritual sustenance, for him it will cause madness.'"

During the last part of this story we had been driving through the streets of Sucre, now empty, for people there go to bed early. The lights glimmered and at the end of a street I could see an almost full moon rising.

"I hope you have enjoyed the day," Don Miguel said as we drew up in front of the Hostal Cruz de Popayán. "Another time I can tell you more stories."

I yawned, got out of the car, reached back in for my extra sweater.

"Thank you, Don Miguel," I said. "Perhaps there will be another time. I hope so. Meanwhile that last story had a modern moral, don't you think?"

Don Miguel laughed. "Perhaps." He got out of the car to escort me to the Hostal door. "I hope you write it in your book."

La Paz

The snowy-white cathedral of Arequipa

PERU
A Group of One

•*Arequipa*

Peruvian textile

In Arequipa work
seems far away,
strife farther, with
every day a time of
leisure and enjoyment.
It is a place of
scarlet geraniums,
white walls and
black iron grill work.

To visit Arequipa, the White City, I returned from La Paz to Lima. I could have gone back to Puno and thence by train toward the coast, but time was growing short on this particular trip, and I didn't want to retrace any steps.

In Lima I approached the airline for a ticket — $150 round trip. In order to pay for it I went out to find a *casa de cambio* where I could change a travelers check. In these South American countries one never uses a bank, I'm not sure why. The exchange office was part of a travel agency, small and friendly, no crowd, so I got in conversation with Señor Vertiz, the manager. I admired the poster of Arequipa with the volcano Misti in the background. It hung on the wall over Señor Vertiz' head, so that the mountain seemed an extension of his thick black hair out of which volcano smoke was belching.

He looked me over critically. "Going to Arequipa? Why don't you go with a group? Cheaper and more secure."

"I don't want a group. I like to travel alone and security doesn't seem to be a problem."

"You could be a group of one."

On my first trip to Peru I had been with two friends and I knew the possibility of bargains for groups of three, or even two, but a group of one?

Later I looked up "group" in the dictionary: two or more of anything ... atoms, languages, stratefied rock, Army battalions.

"Yes?" I said.

"We'll get to that later. You will be well cared for, as a group, by my partners in Arequipa, at Sensational Tours. Meanwhile ..." He looked me over again. "You're American, I suppose? Of course you are. But do you know that the Peruvian airlines let Peruvians travel for much less?" I shook my head.

"Maybe we could make you Peruvian for a little while?" Señor Vertiz smiled ingratiatingly. "I agree," he said, although I had not said anything, "you'd never pass at the airline office, even though your

Spanish is not bad, but you could be Peruvian on the telephone."

"My accent . . ." I murmured.

"*My* accent." Señor Vertiz picked up the phone and made me an instant resident of Peru. "That will be $75 you just saved," he said. "Half the fare. Now about your tour of one in Arequipa . . . that will cost you exactly $75.00."

***

I was met in Arequipa, in my group of one status, by Juan, head of the Sensational Travel Agency. He selected me without hesitation out of the crowd emerging from the plane, and waved enthusiastically as I descended the landing ramp. He grabbed my bag, escorted me to his broken-down car(practically all cars in Peru are veterans.) "Welcome to Arequipa, Señora Celia," he said, and I felt welcome.

"How did you know me in all that crowd?" I asked.

"It was easy. I was looking for *you.*"

***

Arequipa, with 400,000 inhabitants, is the second largest city in Peru, after Lima with its five million. But Arequipans resent being told that theirs is the "second" city. They are fiercely individualistic and have at times even tried for independence. The city seems small and very Spanish with its chalk-white buildings, colonnaded walks and steepled churches. The altitude is reasonable here, about 7,500 feet, and the town can be explored by a visitor without panting and stopping at every corner for a rest. It is green, after the earth shades of the altiplano. There are few remnants of Inca times. This project was strictly colonial and very handsome it is too.

Arequipa is surrounded by farming land, where garlic and onions are the big crops, mostly for export to the United States. These, along with alfalfa, are grown on the *andenes,* those steeped terraces so plentiful around Cuzco. Here they are brilliant green plantings braced by gray walls, in the manner of a formal 18th century French garden rising gracefully in concentric rows to the tops of hillsides. Three volcanoes,

Chanchani, Pichu Pichu, and El Misti, all of them in the 20,000 foot range, loom in the background, while ocean beaches are only a couple of hours drive away.

Arequipa's Plaza de Armas, its arcades strengthened against earthquakes

The White City gets its name from its buildings which are almost all of dazzling sillar stone quarried from the Misti valcano. The Plaza de Armas, the central square, with its huge cathedral and two-storied arcades, is like an immense sugary confection. It is soft, without the harsh toughness of the landscape and architecture of Cuzco. Since soft sillar lends itself to elaborate carving most of the numerous churches are exceedingly baroque.

In Arequipa work seems far away, strife farther, with every day a time of leisure and enjoyment. It is a place of scarlet geraniums, white walls and black iron grill work. There are few Inca relics, although in preconquest times it was a stop on the route from the ocean to Cuzco, when *chasqui* runners brought fresh fish to the Inca's table in twenty-four hours. Most of the historic structures have been repaired at various times because the region is especially susceptible to earthquakes. The restoration is harmonious. One would not know that the twin spires of the cathedral are made, not of sillar stone, but of special light, quake-resistant materials, while in the Plaza de Armas the upper rows of white arches in the *portales* were added in an attempt to make the colonnades earthquake-proof.

Most interesting is the Santa Catalina Convent, a city of nuns dedicated to Saint Catherine of Siena. Established in 1579, the convent was closed to outsiders for four hundred years until, in 1970, it was finally opened to the public. In its heyday several hundred women passed their lives there in a completely equipped secluded town with streets, patios, gardens, chapels, dormitories, laundries, kitchens. Even now a few of the nuns remain in a concealed corner of the settlement. The convent is rich in art, with a large museum and many paintings on the walls of rooms and passages.

When I went to visit the convent, I was surprised to receive, not a flimsy paper ticket of admission, but a large square of wood like a child's building block. It had the number 13 on it.

"What's this?" I asked the woman behind the ticket window. "A good luck piece?"

"It's to let you out," she explained. I had visions of being immured with the few remaining nuns. Later I learned that this colonial monument is unique in that a ticket is more important to get out than to get in. Some years ago a group of visitors hid inside until nightfall, then lowered paintings over the wall to accomplices. These works of art later showed up in New York galleries.

Arequipa is an exceptionally friendly city. It does not have the bustle of an important tourist center, and it's not hard to join a group of local people for a trip to the suburbs to eat a *picantería*, where highly spiced seafood is washed down with chicha drunk from a beaker passed around the table.

The city seemed peaceful, making me wonder why it should be a community of lawyers. I noticed that the streets around the central square were placarded with signs reading *abogado*. I counted fifty in one block. I asked Juan about it.

"There are about two thousand lawyers in this city," he said,"but what they find to litigate about I don't know. They're mostly looking for work."

Everything is far cheaper in Arequipa than in Lima. It's a good place to shop for alpaca goods and leather bags, or to have shoes made to order.

The city is also a good starting point for a long day's journey by car to the altiplano, which rises to 15,000 feet or more on the way to Cuzco. The drive culminates at the Canyon de Colca, a gorge carved out by

Canyon de Colca

running water working for centuries on volcanic rock, until its depth is twice that of the Grand Canyon. On the altiplano, as in other parts of the high country, Quechua-speaking Indians, living in tiny villages of thatch-covered huts, tend their llamas in windswept, desolate pampas country. Here condors pass majestically overhead, and herds of vicuñas graze, keeping a careful distance from humans.

The llamas in these uplands look like prehistoric inhabitants of a great waste of treeless mountains, plains and gorges. Travelers have always been impressed by these animals, ever since the conquistadors first thought of them as a new variety of sheep. Pizarro thought it worth while taking one back with him to Spain, and all chroniclers described them, showing a respect which they did not feel for other animals.

Carletti, a 16th century traveler, wrote, "These are very domestic animals, simple and peaceful, but so extraordinarily stubborn and headstrong that they will move along only in their own way and at their own wish. Feeling weary, or having some other humor, they throw themselves down to lie on the ground even if they have burdens on their backs, and it is impossible to make them get up again even if one wants to kill them, such is their obstinacy. For this reason a custom has arisen of saying to a stubborn person, 'You are a llama.'"

Another writer speaks of "the llamas . . . making little grunts of private conversation among themselves; quite haughty yet so timid with all they are easily guided in droves of fifty by a couple of diminutive Indians."

The llama is an ideal animal for the altiplano, where cactus gives liquid that makes up for the lack of water, and his spongy hooves

Two llamas on the altiplano

allow him to pass over ice. A group of llamas usually consists of one male to about ten females. He protects his herd, keeping watch and, if he sees any danger, he stamps his feet and utters a shrill cry. At least this is what S. S. Hill reported in his story of a journey to Peru in 1860. He suggested that llamas be introduced to Scotland where, however, there would be a scarcity of cactus. Llamas were used to transport

CORREGIMIENTO
COREG^{oz}AFRENTAAL
al ual se hor senaao por sos guabos que no la sa mi hay o.

Beating an Indian

loads but not as mounts for humans. Some of the Spaniards got around this difficulty by employing hardy mountain Indians as *caballitos* or little horses, to carry them up to the steep grades.

Baron Alexandre von Humboldt wrote with disgust of this practice: "Every morning they allow themselves to be saddled, and leaning on a short stick they carry their masters on their backs. Some of them are recommended to travelers as being sure-footed and possessing an easy and even pace; it really makes one's blood boil to hear the qualities of a human being described in the same terms as would be employed in speaking of a horse or mule."

***

The three days of my group-of-one tour flew by with visits to surrounding towns, an excursion to the Canyon de Colca, a chicha and guinea pig party in the country. Often Isabelle from the tourist bureau joined us, or Juan's brother, Jorge. I felt that I had lived in Arequipa always, and began to think about where I would settle when I moved south to spend the rest of my life there. I have hypothetically spent the rest of my life in a number of places, but this one was in the top rank.

After the three days were up I stayed on in the city passing time with my new friends. Somehow I was absorbed into the agency as an unoffical member, going to the airport to meet arriving groups, being assigned to drag the Italian lady out of bed when it was time to start a morning excursion, intervening with the young Frenchmen who insisted that their suitcase, which had unfortunately fallen off a taxi, be mended free by the agency. "But it's Sunday," Juan argued. "The stores aren't open." He didn't say, "The agency is not obliged to mend your suitcase." I offered my English to all who needed it, and even essayed a bit of French.

I now discovered how the travel agents of Arequipa recognize their clients arriving from Lima. We went to meet Señora Mendez of Mexico City, due with her daughter on the afternoon plane.

"How will you know her?" I asked Juan, as we took up our stand at the plate glass window facing the airfield.

"She's fat, ugly, red hair. Blond daughter with her, fourteen years old, pink dress, not bad looking."

I stared at him, inquiringly.

"Easy. They phone us from Lima with a description. Excuse me, there she is." He hurried forward to meet the couple, his smile telling them that in Arequipa, from the Sensational Agency, they would receive the greatest welcome of their entire trip.

Señora Mendez bustled out the gate, waited to locate her six pieces of baggage, and kept an eye on her daughter who had struck up a conversation with a young Colombian tourist.

After introductions, hand shakings, and expressions of pleasure, we went out to the car.

"Now," said Señora Mendez, settling herself in the front seat by Juan, "You must tell me how you recognized me from way across that great big airfield." She fluttered her eyelashes and adjusted her skirt.

"Señora," Juan said, giving her an innocent sideways glance. "It was easy. I was looking for *you.*"

I never inquired what my arrival description had been.

***

Between forays with the Sensational Agency I read books about Arequipa. I learned that, while the city looks wholly Spanish, its foundations, though no longer physically visible like those in Cuzco, go back to mysterious civilizations thousands of years ago, when the population lived by hunting the guanaco and the American ostrich. By the tenth century AD, however, there were evidences of

Tiahuanacu civilization, immigrants arriving from far away Titicaca, and after that time, little by little sculptured *andenes* appeared on the gently rolling hills, more spectacular here than in Cuzco, for here the soil was richer, the vegetation greener. Corn, potatoes and quinoa grew well. Ceramics were made, corpses and mummies were interred in the caves and burial grounds of the green hills.

The Incas settled here in the 15th century, in the time of the emperor Tupac Yupanqui, and the city became a way station for goods imported from the tropical coast. In 1535 the first Europeans entered the valley under command of Ruy Diaz on his way to Chile for a rendezvous with Diego de Almagro. The Spaniards started a settlement here in 1540, attracted by the fact that "in ten months that many Spaniards had lived there, no one had died, and very few Indians."

I tried to write down my impressions, but this has always been difficult for me when I am traveling. It's easier recalled later. Still, I felt guilty, especially when I read Cieza's boast: "Oftentimes when the other soldiers were reposing I was tiring myself by writing ... Neither fatigue nor the ruggedness of the country nor the mountains and rivers, nor intolerable hunger kept me from this task." That's fortunate, or we would know much less than we do about the New World of his time.

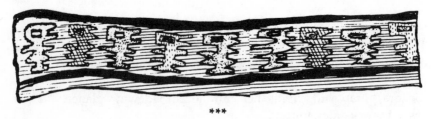

***

When it came time to leave, my farewell to Arequipa was in reverse of my other airport experiences in South America. I nearly missed the flight because it left early. We galloped through the airport, Juan and Isabelle at my side, yelling, "Wait! Wait!"

I almost wish I had missed the plane. Arequipa would be a fine place to live.

Arequipa—children with lambs

Otavalo Indians weave traditional designs

ECUADOR

Two Faces of Quito

•*Quito*

Quito

I arrived in Quito with no preformed ideas. I left it with several impressions. Of course it is breathtakingly beautiful. It is historic and yet, in its new half, the most modern-looking capital I've seen.

"**O**h, man: If ever thou hast the vanity to think thyself more than thou really art, a mere worm upon the earth, or that thou are superior to any other of thy fellow-worms, crawling here below — go, in the depth of winter, and view the tremendous cordillera." Lieutanent Charles Brand of the English Royal Navy wrote his description of the Andes in 1827, during the age of fulsome romantic expression.

I didn't view the peaks of Ecuador in the winter, but, even in October, I could see what the Lieutenant meant. And he did not have the advantage of approach by air, when he would have viewed the lofty snow-clad peaks thrusting their summits through strata of clouds.

These mountains - *Chimborzao, Pichincha, Cotopaxi* - are refuges for hummingbirds who live nowhere else. There are two hundred kinds of hummingbirds with such names as SUn Angels, Incas, Emeralds, Topazes, Green Hermits, Violet Ears, Flame Throwers.

Ecuador is not, however, such a comfortable home for llamas and alpacas as Oeru. There is a double rainy season in the country, with wet rain forests as high as 10,000 feet, up to the snow line, where llamas cannot find their favorite yehu grass for grazing. Since these beasts of burden were unavailable it was said that the Spanish conquerors, their minds ever attracted to precious metals, shod their horses with silver, and even with the harder gold, though whether this made the animals more surefooted on the trails is not recorded.

Quito is 9,400 feet up, sunny and temperate. I approached it from the air, for I had decided to make this country a separate excursion. I arrived, after another of those all night flights from Mexico City, at dawn, the time when, the Incas believed, the sun rises after a night-long swim beneath the earth.

Dropping down among the mountains that surround Quito the plane skimmed low over the suburbs to land perilously on the runway in this second highest capital city airport of South America — only La Paz is higher. The city nestles in a valley among the volcanic peaks. The air is brisk, often chilly, even though the equator is only a few miles away. Traffic moves briskly too, and the people of Quito are inclined to talk rapidly, without the languor which one finds at lower altitudes in this tropical part of the world. The sun shines almost every day and the weather is hardly worth discussing since it is always much the same in an area perched at the dividing point of the world, neither south nor north.

Although Ecuador is small, with eight million inhabitants, and covers an area of less than 300,000 square kilometers, it has all the variety to be found in the topography of its larger neighbors, Peru to the south, Colombia to the north. Guayaquil on the Pacific coast is a sweltering, busy port, shipping bananas, coffee, cocoa to far countries. The Orient, to the east as its name implies, is jungle country where the Napo River runs down to join and enlarge the Amazon, where Indian tribes are still isolated from civilization, and where recent oil discoveries have made Ecuador comparatively rich. In the center of the country is the Sierra, with its capital, Quito, in a land of mountains, rivers and fertile valleys. Snowcovered smoking *Cotopaxi*, at over 19,000 feet, is the world's highest active volcano.

I looked forward to spending a month in Ecuador partly because I seldom read anything about it. Brazil, Peru, Columbia, all have well-publicized economic and political problems. Ecuador, though it has some problems, is compartively quiet about them. It has been a democracy since 1979. Bananas, mining, fishing, recently discovered petroleum are what Ecuador is known for, and I soon found that petroleum is responsible for one of the two faces of Quito...the modern one.

Roads in Ecuador are now good, but in the time of Baron Alexander von Humboldt's explorations (1799 to 1804) the difficulties of travel were so tremendous that it took him and his friend Bonplan four months for the journey from Bogotá to Quito, along a road so narrow that mules were sometimes unable to follow its precipitous windings. When travelers from opposite directions met, one party had to retreat or else climb up the cliff, hanging by roots and outcroppings until the others had passed below them.

My entry into the capital was surely not that difficult, and a friendly taxi driver drove me, for no more than twice the proper fare, to the modest Hotel Auca, in the old city, where life would be less luxurious but more interesting than in the modern quarter. The front door of the hotel was impassable, the lobby full of young men milling about. The mob — no other word for it — ran out into the street, easily brushing me aside, and I went in to register.

"Trouble in town?" I suggested.

The desk clerk looked up in surprise. "Certainly not. A tour party from Colombia. We give them very special rates."

By staying a week I too got a special rate: 10% off the usual charge of $8.00 a night. I also had time to become adept at hotel management, at least how to handle this hotel. When there was hot water there were no towels since they were all in the laundry; when the clean towels arrived the water had been shut off. No problem to hide a towel each day, although explaining the predicament to the chamber maid was impossible. Operating the elevator had its enigmatic charms. Several times I asked the desk clerk for help since the lift refused to rise except at his command. Once, when he was out, I had to climb four flights. Finally, I observed that the elevator would start only when the passenger had closed the door and then kicked it at a spot about a foot above the floor and six inches from the left side. Starting upward with this maneuver gave me a feeling of real power. On arrival at my room I reclined on the bed from which I could look out the picture window at the larger-than-life statue of the Virgin of the Americas on Panecillo Hill above the city. Then I felt the relaxed calm which successful travel gives me.

***

The old city, where I made my headquarters, has retained its colonial charm, which dates back to its reconstruction by the Spanish in 1534. The church of San Francisco dominates an enormous square a block or so away from the Plaza de Independencia with the cathedral and the government palace. In the maze of narrow, ancient streets the traffic is fortunately one way. Pedestrians mingle with cars and trucks, because vendors, selling everything from brassieres to bibles, have spread out until there is no room to use the sidewalks, especially since they are also crowded with agile Ecuadoreans who have mastered the art of making progress against opposition. Surely Quito's million inhabitants are all congregated, all day long, downtown.

Lining the streets of the old city are dozens of four hundred year old houses, and impressive churches, as well as small alleyways and ample courtyards.

I liked my lodgings at the Auca because they were close to scenes of photographic interest. The tripod for my camera was a crowd pleaser. Children and adults swarmed around to watch me set it up, aim for a shot, take a picture. Some wanted to pose, others wanted to chat, still others, especially children, found it fun to intrude on a scene at the last moment. I took to getting up and arriving at the square just after dawn, before even the shoeshine boys had set up business.

The modern Quito, its other face, is something else. Crossing the line between the two districts I was instantly in a city of wide boulevards, handsome shops offering imported and domestic articles in the high price range. Here well dressed people walked at a normal pace along uncluttered sidewalks. Brand new high-rise buildings were all around, housing deluxe hotels with gambling casinos and offices where international trade appeared to be booming. There were all-glass buildings, buildings with no glass, triangular and hexagonal constructions, mushrooms on stilts, architectural forecasts of some outlandish future. Beyond the business district condominiums and apartments had proliferated with more going up. It looked like a forest of towers, but the legal limit was twenty stories high. It may be that no one wants to look down on the volcano Cotopaxi.

Tourists often stay in Quito for a day or two only, taking a city tour, going the fifteen miles out of town to *mitad del mundo*, where they can be photographed standing with one foot on the north side and other other on the south of the equator. I found there was more to the city than a short layover. I enjoyed spending mornings in ancient Quito, its historical landmarks untouched, and then finding myself, after a short taxi ride, in an ultramodern setting for my choice of restaurants of international quality.

I was assured that the modern half of Quito is quite new. Not much more than a decade ago it was all empty fields. *Viva petroleo.*

I was shown a *barrio bajo*, a ghetto area, when I asked if the poor people of Quito had any place to live other than downtown streets. Compared to the horrible slums surrounding other cities it looked middle class. My guide was amazed when I asked if the houses had plumbing, electricity, water. "Of course," he said. The rate of unemployment in Ecuador is, however, high. It was over 20% when I was there, and the indigenous population in rural areas is probably not counted.

Chifas in South America are Chinese restaurants, numerous and popular in Peru and Ecuador. They are sometimes good, sometimes bad, and those in Quito's old town must regretfully be labeled bad. Their specialty, and sometimes their only offering, was *chaulfan*, a heap of rice with miscellaneous and often unidentifiable scraps of meat, egg, vegetables, arranged on top. More tasty, in the Ecuadorean cuisine, is *cuy*, guinea pig cooked whole on a spit, on which it looks sadly vulnerable and defenseless. No, not a pet here, I reminded myself; here it's a basic food. It tasted a bit like chicken.

Another speciality of the country is *sangre de borrego*, sheeps blood fried in parsley, peppers, rice and potatoes. For a party, I was told nothing can take the place of *hornado:* suckling pig baked whole without skinning, adorned with a bell pepper in its mouth and two chile peppers for eyes. This companionable dish is washed down with *leche de tigre*, tiger's milk — punch laced with aguardiente, replacing the ubiguitous chicha of Peru and Bolivia.

Quito is a cultural center. During my time there I heard a symphony concert, watched the Bulgarian ballet, and saw the *Three Penny Opera* given in Spanish.

I used Quito as a base for visits to mountain villages and Indian markets. A trip through the high country of Ecuador reminded me of a child's picture book in vibrant color. The countryside seemed more initmate than the desolate reaches of Peru; proper for a small country. The snow-white conical peaks looked aritficial, an artist's rendering of a locale where witches and goblins roam. After the modern city of Quito I was startled by the sudden complete change to an Indian landscape. Against the backgroup of blue sky and silvery mountains green checkerboard fields were turned up on end, alternating with almost vertical brown squares of raw earth where oxen worked the land dragging primitive plows. Men labored in the fields, women trudged along the country roads, in their wide skirts, shawls, white top hats, with the ever-present spindle of wool turning busily in their hands.

Black-and-white Holstein cattle moved slowly across grazing land. In the country villages I passed thatched-roofed houses protected from evil by small white crosses on the roof-trees; wooden fretwork decorated windows and doors. The eucalyptus trees looked as though they had been tastefully arranged by a landscape architect to tower over the fields; while the lower "African trees" were reminiscent of scenes in movies of the veldt where zebras and hartebeests should roam.

The equator

To me the equator, in spite of the expensive monument erected to the *Mitad del Mundo*, seemed unimpressive, unimaginative. I preferred to think of the imaginery line which ran beneath the monument. The mapping of the equator through South America had been a project occupying many years and the best efforts of scientists. Now it makes a handy brief excursion for tour leaders, so that flocks of tourists from all corners of the world, north or south of the monument, can snap cameras and buy postcards and souvenirs in the gift shop.

Side trips from any South American city are a simple matter. Take a bus, hire a car, or join a tour. I tried both bus and tour car, the latter never really a tour in the sense of a large group of people. A car would pick me up, after I had agreed to pay whatever I could lower the price to, and we would then stop for one or two other people who shared the cost. Quito was not crowded with tourists when I was there in late September and early October. The weather was always beautiful, not much rain, no excessive heat, no problem of any sort.

A little boy in the Otavalo market

My trip to the Indian weaving center at Otavalo, made on a tour arrangement with a couple of other foreigners, was of more than tourist interest. The Saturday market was a proof that some Indian tribes have survived the domination of the white man with their dignity intact. They weave blankets, ponchos, sweaters, and have either adopted from Europeans or perhaps have always possessed a strong economic sense. They often operate modern textile factories, but they continue also with traditional ways, wearing their white trousers, ponchos and felt hats. Their commercial success assures them respect from Ecuadorean society, but they refuse to give up their racial identity. Their typical costume includes braids for both women and men. The men are subject to army draft but are now permitted, after their sharp protest at haircutting, to retain their braids while in the service.

My side trip to Santo Domingo de los Colorados was made by bus, a tremendous downhill ride from high country to a land of palms, tropical flowers and noonday heat. I went there following a statement in my guidebook that there would be the Colorado Indians, dressed almost entirely in stripes painted on their skins — a good subject for photographs, surely. Santo Domingo was disappointing in all respects. It rained, the market was undistinguished, and no striped warriors were to be seen. A taxi driver did offer to drive me to the "chief's house."

"Where does he live?" I asked, hopefully.

"Oh, he has a good house in the suburbs. He's a very friendly person, always glad to see strangers." Fearing a real let-down with a chief in a condo or a town house I refrained from looking him up.

***

I arrived in Quito with no preformed ideas. I left it with several impressions. Of course it is breathtakingly beautiful. It is historic and yet, in its new half, the most modern-looking capital I've seen.

Plaza Independencia, Quito

There's something else besides. It is the spirit of the city, which seems self-contained, undisturbed, floating in another and a happier time frame. I may very well be wrong and some tragedy may be brewing. Meanwhile, I like the English translation in a local tourist brochure: "Without bragging Quito has the charisma of its intimate personality. It looks great, picturesque, calm and kind. This is for sure the emotion Quito reserves for tourists." For sure it is.

Street scene in Quito

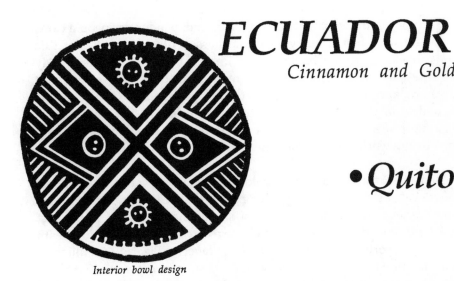

ECUADOR

Cinnamon and Gold

Interior bowl design

•Quito

*There was the fabled kingdom
of El Dorado, the Golden Man,
where gold was so common
that the king wore only
a fine coating of gold dust.
This outfit was washed
from his body every night,
and replaced with a fresh coat
the next morning, applied
over a sticky layer of
sweet-smelling resin.*

In the central square of Quito, Plaza Independencia, people came and went, some hurrying to businesses, others offering for sale shoelaces, comic books, small images of Saint Francis, gaudy picture postcards. The Pinquino man pushed his ice cream cart around, and from the flagpole of the government building the Ecuadorean flag fluttered jauntily in the breeze. I sat on a bench, resting in the morning sun and considering this city's history, surely one of the world's most romantic.

When the Pizarro brothers arrived from Spain, it was still a time of medieval romance and they, along with their companions, expected to experience in real life the sort of stories they had read in the best sellers of Amadis de Guala, which stirred readers' imaginations with tales of all sorts of mystical far places. Francisco Pizarro was illiterate, but he must certainly have heard these romances in his home province of Estremadura, an arid Spanish district which lacked excitement.

The Pizarro brothers did live romantic tales in real life, with chivalry eliminated and tragedy added. They had little basic information about the New World and no way to sift true rumors from false. This made their expeditions more exciting; also, when they failed, more tragic.

During the early days, in the 16th century, Quito saw much coming and going of recently arrived Spaniard. They left the mountain city proudly, with banners waving, horses caracoling, retainers suitably burdened and subservient.

They returned, when they returned at all, in rags, starving, their eyes sombre with memories of gruesome battles and horrible suffering. The longed-for discovery of El Dorado and its golden king was unattained, the Land of Cinnamon and impractical project, where the harvesting would bring no financial rewards. It was hard to decide which was more menacing, the high country, bare, freezing cold, with hazardous cliff-hanging trails, or the hot land of the rain forest, where creepers and vines made horse travel impossible, where insects were everywhere, anacondas dropped from branches overhead, hostile Indians sprang out from ambush.

However, Gonzalo Pizarro, when he rode into the province of Quito, had profit, not misfortune, in mind. In Europe any story about the newly discovered western land was believable and much was true. There was that Land of Cinnamon, for instance. Spain needed spices, a source of wonderful profit for the Protuguese traders who had a monopoly on the spice market in the Orient. There were persistent rumors of great forests of cinnamon on the south of Quito. A fortune to be made. Gonzalo Pizarro set out to find them.

His expedition left Quito in February, 1541, a band of 220 Spaniards on horseback, each man carrying his bag of provisions, his gun and ammunition. Everything else was transported by "inferiors." Lines of pack animals marched sedately along the way, accompanied by 2,000 hogs, and 4,000 Indians, most of whom would die in the Amazon jungles. The native slaves were kept chained until departure to prevent them from running off into the mountains. (Yet the chronicler Zarate referred to them as "Indian friends" and Pizarro in a letter to the King of Spain wrote of the "Indians who went joyfully.") With the explorers, also, went a pack of 2,000 enormous savage hunting dogs, to be used for fighting, hunting, torture of captured enemies, or food if it came down to that. They would be handy to subdue hostile Indians along the way — the Spaniards called this "dogging them."

The expedition met difficulties almost immediately. Dozens of Indian bearers died in the mountain cold, and then the party reached an area near the Amazon where horses could not penetrate the forest. Rain blinded the riders and soaked their equipment. Herds of animals were nothing but a hindrance here.

Richard Spruce, who took the same route 300 years later, described the still rugged way: "Road there is none, but only the merest semblance of a track, such as a tapir makes to its feeding and drinking places, often carried along the face of precipices, where had it not been for projecting roots on which to lay hold, the passage would have been impossible . . .The rains set in with greater severity than ever... the dripping forest through which I had to push my way, soaking my garments so that towards evening my arms and shoulders were quite benumbed and the mud ... was often over the knees."

Later Pizarro wrote to the Spanish King, "After seventy days during which we endured great hardships ... we found the trees which bear cinnamon, which is in the form of flower buds ... the leaf has the flavor also but not the bark. It is a commodity by which Your Majesty cannot be rendered service."

During the journey to the Land of Cinnamon the Spaniards, not to mention the Indians, encountered horrors never dreamed of in the tales of Amadis de Gaula. The problems were so great that one writer of the time described them as "such that anyone but Gonzalo Pizarro would have abandonded such an Enterprise as seems to be opposed by both Heaven and Earth."

Zarate tells us, "There happened a marvailous great Earthquake with rayne and tempest of Lightning and Thunder, and the ground opened in many places, and swallowed up more than 500 houses ... They finally reached the Province of Sumao where the Zinamon grows, with leaves like until bay leaves ... where the fruit groweth like until a great acorne ... He returned back again to Quito, from whence he had traveled more than 400 leagues of most evill way, among Mountaynes, and country unhabited ... where 40 of his men ended their days, without any hope of succour but even as they asked for meate ...they fell downe dead with hunger ... They killed their horses which were left, and greyhounds with other sort of dogs to eat ... Their clothes were torred from their bodies so that now, each of them had but only two small deare skins, which covered their fore parts and also their hinder partes."

Other chronicles reveled in the grim details of starvation. Pizarro's men bled their horses once a week and used their helmets to cook up a meal of blood and herbs. Then they turned to lizards, frogs and roots. Along the way they consumed more than a thousand dogs and a hundred horses. Finally they were eating nothing but leather belts and soles of shoes. It was said that toward the end of the journey the explorers died at the rate of four to a mile.

These were the sufferings of the Spaniards, who wished to consider themselves at this point in their lives, hidalgos, "sons of somebody", although they had started life illegitimate, poor, and without worldy prospects. What happened to the Indians, how many of the 4,000 starved, and with what agonies, the Spaniards do not describe.

***

Sitting there in Plaza Independencia, I thought of the Pizarro expedition of 1541 outward bound, fired by a fierce desire to become rich, to live down the past, to be somebody. They marched away with banners flying, horses prancing, while the riders, proud as they had never been in the badlands of Spain, walked their mounts "at a Castilian pace" —whatever that may have been. I imagined the thousands of Indians, the hundreds of horses, the dogs and pigs and lines of pack animals, and the dense crowd of onlookers watching a party of adventurers proceeding into the unknown.

***

Cinnamon was not the only source of riches rumored to exist to the southeast of Quito. There was the fabled kingdom of El Dorado, the Golden Man, where gold was so common that the king wore only a fine coating of gold dust. This outfit was washed from his body every night, and replaced with a fresh coat the next morning, applied over a sticky layer of sweet-smelling resin. The monarch considered gold dust more handsome than any suit of clothes. As for gold plates and ornaments —much too awkward, actually vulgar.

Sir Walter Raleigh had searched for this country in his last tragic expedition to the Orinoco. Other explorers, fascinated, crisscrossed the area looking for fabulous wealth. Portuguese from Brazil and Spaniards from New Granada pursued the quest.

Always behind the Spaniards' adventuring there was that one overriding purpose: to amass wealth, to become important, to live down their origins as nobodies. For this they were willing to suffer every hardship. "They thirsted mightily for gold; they wished to stuff themselves with it, they starved for it, lusted for it as pigs do for acorns."

Most thrilling of all were those stories of the Golden Man with his coating of precious dust. A Chibcha Indian legend told of the Lake of Guatavita, on a remote peak in the Colombian Andes where a Princess threw herself into the water, leaving her Prince to mourn for months beside the lake. Finally he asked advice of a sorcerer who instructed him to dive into the ice-cold lake. On coming up he swam to shore and gave the news: "The Princess is alive! She sits in a palace more beautiful than ours where she is happy." Twice a year pilgrims came to the lake. They smeared the body of their chief with balsam resin, blew gold dust on it, and took him to the center of the lake by raft. He tossed gold, emeralds and precious images into the water, then immersed himself until the gold dust was washed away.

Oviedo, an historian of the Indies, wrote of El Dorado, as he imagined it: "I would rather have the sweepings from the chamber of this monarch than that of the great melting establishments in Peru or in any part of the world."

There was a factual basis for the El Dorado story. At one time Indians used to throw gold ornaments into a deep lake outside Bogotá once a year, and a priest would be covered with gold dust and washed clean. However, this ceremony ceased long before the Spaniards arrived.

In rumors the site of El Dorado gradually changed its position, moving south toward the Amazon. Its original position was known, however, to some explorers. At one time three separate expeditions, each ignorant of the others, converged on El Dorado. It then turned out that the gold at this genuine El Dorado was not even native to the area, but was all the result of trade — a crushing disappointment to the treasure hunters.

***

A writer of thrillers could not have invented any stories more exciting than those the Spaniards actually lived. There were Amazons, for instance. Were they a real nation of warrior women or was the story a fabrication? There were detailed reports:

"With their bows and arrows in their hands they do as much fighting as ten men, and there was one woman who shot arrows a span deep into one of the brigantines; until he looked like a porcupine."

The chronicler Carvajal described the fighting women as "very white and tall and having hair long and braided and wound about the head, and they are very robust and go about naked, but with their privy parts covered." These women were said to live in the interior of the country where they ruled several provinces. Their villages, built of stone, were inhabited only by women. They would make war on a neighboring tribe and capture husbands for themselves. They raised their female children and trained them as warriors, but male offspring were killed and their bodies returned to their fathers.

The Amazons had much gold and silver, it was said, and draped themselves in beautiful blankets, sometimes wearing golden crowns. Animals, like camels in appearance, carried them about. When they parted from their men they gave them green jade-like stones, "Amazon stones." These are sometimes still found in that area.

Amazon women were often present in Indian folklore and, subtracting some of the exotic details, there may well have been such tribes. At any rate many future explorers believed in their existence.

***

I walked across the plaza to photograph a plaque on the wall of the cathedral. It had been placed there "in memory of Francisco Orellana, discoveror of the Amazon."

Gonzalo Pizarro found none of the fabulous riches he sought, but Orellano, one of his subordinates, discovered and journeyed down the greatest river in the world. It brought him no gold, nothing but suffering and the immortaility of that plaque, bearing his name, in the principal square of the ancient city of Quito.

On the way to the market—Cuenca

ECUADOR

The Athens of Ecuador

CÍVDAD
LACÍVDADDEQVENCA

Cuenca

•*Cuenca*

*At the hotel I was
charmed by day
with the view of the
Tomebamba River,
the colonial buildings
beyond it, and beyond
them mountains and a sky
where clouds changed
formation in a continual
slow dance. At night
I fell asleep to the music
of water rippling
briskly over stones
just below my window.*

My last afternoon in Quito it rained. Since I was reading a book of traditional poems I looked for a historical viewpoint. Here it was:

> *The skies of Quito*
> *Are treacherous like a woman ...*
> *From Quito to Heaven,*
> *And in Heaven a little hole*
> *To look down at my Quito...*
> *There's no sky like that of Quito*
> *But only for a downpour!*

My translation might not be very poetic but the idea came through ...wet weather likely.

However, the next morning was clear for my departure to Cuenca, a Colonial city which I thought would probably interest me for three days or so. The guidebooks hadn't much to say about it except "good water," "not well coordinated for tourism," and - an adjective which attracted me - "convivial."

In the hotel coffee shop I ate a continental breakfast, which is what you get in South America unless you insist on something else, refused an offer of a last dish of *chaulafan,* and went up to my room for my baggage, giving the elevator a farewell kick on the way.

Cuenca is only a 35 minute flight from Quito, while by road through the mountains the journey takes twelve hours. The time passed quickly. I looked out the window at the familiar panorama and white peaks of whiter clouds below, accepted a Coca Cola from the flight attendant, and looked around at my fellow passengers, most of them businessmen with brief cases, bound for Cuenca, which is Ecuador's third largest city. I did see a fellow American who attracted my attention, since in the parts of South America where I have been they are rather scarce: a young woman with a back pack and a painter's easel. I was curious, but not curious enough to change my seat to be near her.

I asked a Cuenca businessman sitting beside me where to stay. "The Hotel Crespo," he told me. "Be sure to ask for a room looking on the Tomebamba River."

Cuenca, like Quito, is a high Sierra city. We descended through the clouds, skimmed over a mountain, the plane shuddered as the pilot jammed on the brakes, and we barreled to a successful landing on the runway, which would just accommodate a modern jet. A new Canadian-built type of plane, holding fifty passengers and stopping in a very short space, was successfully tried out while I was in Cuenca. I hope it has been put in operation. Such a plane would cut down, not only on accidents, but on heart attacks of passengers.

We entered the airport and I again noticed the young American woman, lugging her backpack and easel, but my reactions were slow. Immediately afterwards I thought, I should have approached her and passed the time of day.

I went to the Hotel Crespo, as recommended, and the young woman arrived almost simultaneously. Carol and I spent the next few days together exploring Cuenca and its environs, she painting, I photographing — an excellent arrangement.

View from my window in Cuenca

At the hotel I was charmed by day with the view of the Tomebamba River, the colonial buildings beyond it, and beyond them mountains and a sky where clouds changed formation in a continual slow dance. At night I fell asleep to the music of water rippling briskly over stones just below my window.

I had planned my Cuenca trip for two or three days only, but after an hour spent exploring the Parque Calderon, the market, and the quiet streets with their ancient buildings, I changed my plans. I made a weekly rate at the Crespo, to stay the remaining three weeks of my vacation there.

Like Quito, Cuenca is cool, even though it is close to the equator. The countryside creeps in near the city. A short taxi ride crossing a couple of the city's four rivers brought Carol and me to open fields and woods. Houses built of adobe with carved wooden balconies and red tile roofs looked out over green, very green checkerboard fields where black-and-white cattle grazed. Along the streams women were washing reeds to be made into baskets and panama hats.

A country town near Cuenca

Carol set up her easel and got to work. I tried for photos but found the women shy, the men too far away across the plowed fields for very good shots. Barking dogs took exception to my camera, so I sat down in a pasture, leaned against a Eucalyptus tree, and opened the book on Cuenca which I had bought at the tourist office. I was pleased by the last sentence of the Dedication: "To those who come from afar to visit this obscure corner of the world and hope to gain something from it." The text, in Spanish and slightly fractured English, told me of all the sights, including Indians in the country "waving"

My rival photographer in the main square of Cuenca

straw hats rather than weaving them, and the admonition that if you have lost your travelers checks and have not recorded the numbers, "It is a piety but it is too late." An English-speaking editor could have a field day in Ecuador. However, the insouciance of the writers' style is part of their charm. Still, should I ever actually move to South America, as I have been tempted to do, surely I could get an editing job at any tourist bureau.

I read that Cuenca had always prided itself on being "The Athens of Ecuador" where poetry was written, paintings painted, music played, and when not otherwise engaged, inhabitants meditated and became philosophers. I was later told by a properly irate Cuenca citizen that some highly placed official in the government had stated, "the troble with Ecuadoreans is that they read too many books." Cuenca, I could see, was a hotbed for such subversion, with its three universities, its *Casa de Cultura*, its frequent book fairs. Even its recently canonized saint, Hermano Miguel, was noted as much for his learning as for his piety. He spent years researching fine points of the Castilian language, in Ecuador and also in Europe.

In 1557 the Spanish founded the city of Santa Ana of the Four Rivers of Cuenca, where the Inca city of Tomebamba had stood, and where Cañari Indians had earlier settled. The Spaniards built a town reported to be "devoid of sumptuous architecture, but constructed of double Castilian adobe, whose yardwide walls are windproof, bullet proof, and gossip proof."

No much went on, in isolated Cuenca, after the Spanish had built up ther settlement, and therefore new arrivals caused a sensation. In 1737, the French Geodetic Mission, which was to map the equator, came to the city and brought excitement and alarm. Very few people understood the reason for their presence. They were believed to be treasure hunters as they made mysterious forays to neighboring towns. However, they were young, adventurous, intelligent, and spoke a foreign language. This lead them to become, for a while, favorites in provincial society. They stayed until 1744 making terrestrial measurements and left behind them influences from European culture which continued until Cuenca's intellectual high point at the end of the 19th century when it earned its name of "Athens."

***

Since Cuenca is about the friendliest city I have ever visited, it soon seemed that I knew a great many people. Once introduced it was a short transition to becoming friends. At the end of a week I had as much trouble as the local folk in making my way down the main strees ... so many acquaintances to greet, shake hands with, discuss my impressions of Cuenca.

While it still feels isolated, Cuenca is not behind the times. By satellite the entire population could watch on television the canonization of their saint. There is money in Cuenca: the biggest business a tire factory, and next to that furniture making. Estimates differed as to how many residents of Cuenca were able to afford the trip to Rome to watch the ceremony at St. Peter's in person. No one guessed fewer than 2,000 and some estimated 15,000. This in a city of less than 200,000 people.

Some older people lament the passing of Cuenca's fame as Athens. "No more," they say. "That's just a matter of history. You should have been here a century ago, when the mystics and philosophers lived among us."

However, immediately after arriving I began to experience the cultural attractions of Cuenca: three openings of art exhibits on my first afternoon. I found none of the work outstanding but the painters were a cosmopolitan lot . . . an American, a Colombian, an Ecuadorean.

Some young writers of the area were just forming a group called "La Palabra" to advance their literary aspirations. They planned to publish a magazine of the same name. At their public poetry reading, the room was packed with an attentive audience, several of whom asked questions afterwards as to style and content.

I enjoyed my three weeks in Cuenca but, to be sure, I missed out on some more exciting adventures — at least so they sounded in the brochures the hotel manager offered me.

There was the "Flotel" which, for a mere few hundred dollars a piece would ferry a group of tourists in luxury down the Napo River through the jungle, provided the water was deep enough. (What would be offered if it wasn't?) Then there would be a trek on foot into the wilds for a night in a comfortable jungle dormitory. On the way there the expedition members would not see any wild animals since they do not appear to large groups of human beings, but the group could all swing along by *lianas* (vines) and know that the beasts in the jungle were watching, no doubt with amazement. At the end of the trip there would be a stop at a small private zoo for picture taking so the travelers could tell stay-at-homes of their adventures.

The other expedition offered three days among the headhunters, the primitive Jívaro (Shuar) Indians. My guidebook told me that now in modern times it would be tactless to ask them about headhunting and shrinking, but the brochure didn't feel that way. It was a few hours drive from Cuenca to Sucua, haunt of the headhunters, and the tour guaranteed that each visitor would come back with his own head. He could even bring another head as a souvenir. It would be the shrunken head of a monkey, which takes three days to prepare, and the results are remarkably lifelike. So much for the posters I had admired in Quito, which proclaimed that no wild animals could be legally killed in Equador.

The hotel manager, who evidently had a stake in both tours, frequently tested Carol and me to see if we had changed our minds, but we had not.

The hills of Ecuador from Ingapirca

"That's the trouble with Americans," I heard him tell one of the waiters. "They just don't know how to travel or what to see."

Carol and I had no trouble finding interesting things and places to see, especially as we were soon joined by Adolfo, a teacher at one of the three universities. On meeting Carol he instantly took a few days off and accompanied us everywhere we went. Since he was an authority on the art and history of the area, this was welcome. He was also welcome since being blonde, as Carol had already discovered, is a risk factor in this brunette part of the world.

We visited the Inca ruins in Ingapirca, the village of San Joaquin where panama hats are made, and the high lagoons of Cajas, where dozens of lakes dot a naked moonlike landscape, a few llamas roam, and fishermen catch the rainbow and salmon trout which the Crespo featured on its menu.

***

It was a half day's drive, over rough dirt roads, to reach the only sizable Inca ruin in Ecuador, Ingapirca, a fortress structure built by Inca Huayna Capac, conqueror of the Cañari tribe. It took the three of us two days actually to arrive at the spot — still not as long as llama herds would have required. We hired a car with a driver for the trip. The car came to a sudden halt at the Tambo station. Whether this was

The station at Tambo

the name of the town or simply a repeat of the Inca word for "inn" I never learned. The derelict hotel and railroad station appeared to be waiting patiently for a non-arriving train, and a rough hand-lettered sign read "Road closed ahead." One of Cuenca's rivers had flooded and taken out a bridge. Next day we hired a jeep instead of a taxi, took a rougher route, and arrived without trouble.

What a far cry from the tourist mobs at Machu Picchu. Here a stray dog, a few placid Holsteins, a woman and little girl gathering greens completed the roster of living things. The guidebook told me that this agreeable isolation, while it has preserved the atmosphere of the hillside, has been detrimental to the site. Local farmers pried boulders from the Inca walls to build stables and barns; tourists picked up smaller rocks as souvenirs. This desecration has recently been stopped, with a guard checking the coming and going of visitors. The ruin had been in its time an important structure. It is still said, by some Indians of the area, that "the sun and moon rise here."

On our way home from Ingapirca we passed through a small town where a fiesta was in progress, with country people arriving on horseback, and a brass band on the church steps rending the air with a fanfare of trumpets in a pervading four-four rhythm. The musicians, not spoiled by too many visitors, were eager to arrange themselves for

Country band, Ecuador

the camera, to grin and joke as to who should be in the limelight, and to prop up one or two artists the worse for celebrating. I recognized a few favorites from the Ecuadorean tapes I had bought: "Sad Heart," "The Romance of My Destiny," "Cuenca Girl," — sad sad songs, sung in a jovial spirit.

***

Carrots and anything else you could want in the Cuenca market

some Latin American markets photography is frowned on as though it might rot the bananas and onions. In the Cuenca market, however, the droll behavior of foreigners is a matter for hilarity. My camera was greeted with enthusiasm, creating crowd scenes where before there had been only token attendance.

***

For my research on the panama hat industry I approached one of Cuenca's various hat factories, and interviewed a third generation hat man, Señor Rodriguez, in his shop. Men and women were busy knotting, washing, bleaching, pressing and packaging all manner of straw hats for export. Señor Rodriguez welcomed an interview and, when it was over, offered me my choice of a hat to wear away.

"Panama hats," as I had already learned, were never made in Panama. Perhaps their name originated because they were worn by workers on the Panama Canal. Their center of manufacture has been Cuenca for more than a century.

A first step in Panama hat weaving

The raw material is prepared on the Ecuadorean coast, in the hot lands, where the *carludovica palmata* palm grows. The shoots are processed into dry whitish fibers which are shipped to the Cuenca area for weaving. Country people, supplementing their small subsistence from agriculture, buy the fiber in the straw market to be worked into hats in their spare time at home. Just before dawn is the best time for weaving, they say, because the night dew makes the straw flexible. The country people bring the hats back semi-finished to the same market and sell them to the dealers for finishing and export.

When hats went out of style in the 1950's, the Cuenca industry slumped badly, but of late years it has been coming back, especially since the straw is now used for other things, such as bags or belts. I didn't tell Señor Rodriguez that I belong to the non-hat wearing generation, but took his gift along for a present to someone who needed shade from the sun.

***

Carol and I found much to see in and around Cuenca until it came time for her return to the United States where a teaching job awaited her. I stayed on another week for I found that daily life was most enjoyable in a city where the visitor can feel at home. Writers of Ecuadorean travel brochures have a knack for describing their country's attractions in an original style. The guidebook advised me to look at the city from a neighboring hill, doing it the native way: stand with my back to the town, lean over and look between my legs. The city would then, the book said, appear to be floating on a cloud. Since that was not a convenient way to take a photograph, I persuaded myself that Cuenca was floating on a cloud anyway. I agreed with the brochure's parting statement: "A social, simple spirit makes of Cuenca, in the province of Azuay, one of the most charming cities of the country."

Bus to Gualaceo

Cuenca farmhouse

ECUADOR

How round is the world?

Inca warrior

The Ecuadoreans couldn't believe what they
were seeing as the Frenchmen set out every day
dragging their weird equipment: theodolites,
barometers, measuring rods, taking care of it all
as if it were made of fragile glass. No high class
Ecuadorean would lead such a rugged life. These
were sophisticated Europeans. Why did they
stare at the stars? There could only be one
anwser: there must be money in it somewhere
The Spanish colony in Quito was certain the
newcomers were after gold. 'Surely no one
could be stupid enough to cross half the world
and spend miserable months in the icy highlands
of the Andes merely to look at the stars and
measure the earth's shape." Who cared
where the equator went on the earth's surface;
it was invisible and that was enough.

A dolfo was a professor of history, specializing in the past of Cuenca and its province of Azuay. So, although I think he skipped a good many of his lectures at the University while he entertained Carol and me, his profession was never far from his thoughts. We learned much more than the guidebooks had told us.

We were lunching at El Jardin, one of Ecuador's best restaurants, tucked away on a back street in Cuenca.

"Did you know I was part French?" Adolfo lifted his glass of wine and smiled lovingly to Carol. "Oh, it's pretty far back, a great great great grandfather actually, but all the stories have come down to me. I didn't have to read any books; I listened to them when I was a child."

"I know the French were here looking for the equator," I remarked. "Sometime in the 18th century. Right?"

"They came to Ecuador in 1734, to Quito first, then Cuenca. I won't tell you which of them was my ancestor for it was a matter of a brief affair." He glanced at Carol, putting on as French an air as he could manage. "It was the French who brought sophistication to Cuenca, the civilized behavior which later caused it to be known as the Athens of Ecuador. But you've heard that, I suppose."

"Yes," Carol said, "but we haven't heard much about the equator, although I went to see it when I was in Quito. Did the geographers have trouble finding it, or what?"

"No they knew where it was, of course. But there were arguments about the shape of the earth."

"Round," I said firmly. "It's round."

"Not completely round. The menu, please, and then we'll have lunch." The waiter hurried to oblige.

"You wouldn't expect that this remote little city of Cuenca in Ecuador would become involved in a scientific struggle bringing in famous names and rival European countries. However, Ecuador was the only place in the whole world which lay on the equator at the accessible spot. So here they finally solved the dispute which raged between

Isaac Newton, the Englishman, and Jacques Cassini, Astronomer Royal of France. National honor was at stake"

Adolfo sipped his wine and went on in his most professional manner.

"Newton proved, theoretically, that the shape of the planet determined the length of the day and that the earth was flattened slightly at the poles and swollen in its middle. He believed that the pull of the moon and sun on the equatorial bulge made the planet wobble like a top. Those Europeans had just about as many ideas about the heavens as the Incas, from whom, of course, I am also descended."

"Cassini, though, backed up by the French Academy of Sciences, was enraged at this theory, since he was convinced that the earth lengthened towards the polar diameter, was longer at the poles, constricted at the equator."

"I've read a good deal of that," I said, "but the details are always interesting. What happened?"

"Newton and his Englishmen were triumphant when Jean Richter went to Guyana with a pendulum clock and found that the pendulum slowed its beat near the equator."

"So what did that mean?" Carol asked.

"It proved, according to Newton, that the earth was an oblate spheroid, flattened at the poles, not a prolate spheriod, as Cassini believed, longer at the poles and constricted at the equator. To prove this one way or another two expeditions set out in 1934, one to Lapland and one to Quito, each to measure the meridian of a degree of latitude. If Newton was correct, the length would increase slightly toward the poles. It wasn't only a matter of national honor; it was essential for drawing correct navigational charts."

At this point our lunch was served, a very French meal. An excellent coquille St. Jacques, green salad, crepes suzette. Adolfo had ordered everything specially, no doubt to impress Carol, but I got to eat it too.

"Well," Adolfo went on, when we had reached the state of after-lunch coffee, "the French Academicians set out under the leadership of Charles-Marie de la Condamine. He was a man of many talents: chronicler, astronomer, cartographer, naturalist. The party included a doctor, a botanist, two mathematicians, a naval captain, a draughtsman, a watchmaker and a young boy, a nephew of the Treasurer of the Academy.

"They had an exhausting journey to Quito since nothing much was known of our country then, at least not in faraway Europe. They reported the discovery of marvels such as a spot where the Indians had once worshipped an emerald the size of an ostrich egg, to which they had dedicated a church. Less glamorous was the wet weather, the rough country, the interminable days of travel. La Condamine's only satisfaction was that he protected his instruments with a rubber cloth he had found along the way.

"On their arrival, soaked, hungry and exhausted at Quito the Frenchmen were at first greeted as heroes. There was a magnificent welcome for the 'measurers of the arc,' with Indians dancing and church bells ringing.

"However, the land around Quito, as both of you must have noticed when you were sightseeing there, was not made for exact measurements. It's full of gulleys and hills and streams and cliffs. The scientists had to mark an exact base line with a six-foot iron bar, from which all their other measurements would be made. The Ecuadoreans couldn't believe what they were seeing as the Frenchmen set out every day dragging their weird equipment: theodolites, barometers, measuring rods, taking care of it all as if it were made of fragile glass. No high class Ecuadorean would lead such a rugged life. These were sophisticated Europeans. Why did they stare at the stars? There could only be one anwser: there must be money in it somewhere. The Spanish colony in Quito was certain the newcomers were after gold. 'Surely no one could be stupid enough to cross half the world and spend miserable months in the icy highlands of the Andes merely to look at the stars and measure the earth's shape." Who cared where the equator went on the earth's surface; it was invisible and that was enough."

Adolfo finished his coffee, called for the bill. "That's the end of the lecture for today," he said, laughing. "Class is called off. Carol and I are going for a walk by the river. Want to come along?" I said no, for the day had turned too dark for picture taking, and besides I had the siesta habit contracted long ago in Mexico. They strolled off hand in hand and I went back to the Crespo.

Adolfo didn't bring the Frenchmen up again, but I did some researching on my own. I found that the subject had been thoroughly written up, especially by members of the expedition. One of the scientists wrote in his journal: "The serenity in which we live on high mountains swept by wind and hail ... the tranquility and constance in which we pass from one scene of desolate solitude to another only feed their suspicions ... Some consider us little better than lunatics. Others impute our whole proceedings to the fact that we are endeavoring to discover some rich mineral or buried treasure ... When we inform them of the real motive of the expedition it causes much astonishment."

In Europe, if not in the New World, this was the Age of Reason. Scientific research had top priority and esteem. There was a belief that all the world's mysteries could be understood, and France was especially concerned with tracing the line of the equator. The Spaniards in South America were dealing with men of intellect and culture, not ignorant adventurers looking for gold.

Tragedies started at once. First, in Quito, the Treasurer's nephew died of fever. Then the scientists were horrified to learn that the Lapland expedition had already proved that Newton's theories were right. However, they decided to continue their research anyway.

They moved on to remote, provincial Cuenca. Here they met even more bafflement and misunderstanding. They made various trips to surrounding towns . . . looking for what? They had authorization for their work from Philip VI, King of Spain — in itself strange, for foreigners were generally banned from any kind of business ventures in the Spanish-owned territories.

However, they were attractive. They became spoiled favorites of local society. The surgeon with the party, Jean Seniergues, made himself available to treat citizens as well as members of the mission. One night, during a house call, he met and fell in love with a daughter of the family, Manuelita, known as "La Cusinga." The doctor became a frequent house guest and quarreled with the girl's previous suitor. The couple scandalized the church authorities with their amorous public behavior. Cuenca was a provincial conservative town, surely not used to the mores of Paris. The affair culminated in August, 1739, at a bullfight in honor of Our Lady of the Snow, in San Sebastian Plaza. A small tiff led to Seniergues, sword in hand, facing the master of ceremonies. The mob quickly took over, yelling "Death to the French Devils." The doctor was beaten up and died three days later.

This was the culminating tragedy. There had been other misfortunes: A servant lost the botanist's entire collection covering five years of work. The scientist suffered a mental breakdown from which he never recovered. One of the draughtsmen died in a fall. The other expedition members met varying fates: two went mad, two married, one took a teaching position at a university. Varied fortunes good and bad, but there was no longer a group or an expedition; only individuals working out their lives. Anyway, since the earth had been proved to bulge at the equator, Isaac Newton had won.

The fact that the French expedition caused a ruckus in Cuenca is now only a romantic memory filled with derring-do: drawn swords, pistols flourished, honor defended and defiled, bravery or cowardice, depending on which side you favored.

The French were not the only people to leave a history of violence in Cuenca. Any guide will point out that the door of the Convent of the Conception is the spot where Zavala the Swordsman expired in 1779. His feud was with Governor Vallejo, who arrived from Spain in 1777 to take over the government. Vallejo immediately noted that Cuena, a frontier city, was "infested with vagrants, gamblers, thieves, and murderers." He proposed to raise the tone for the place by personally confronting all those scoundrels, seeing to it that they were arrested and executed. He set out to do so, hanging the bodies of evil-doers from posts at the entrances to the city, to remind local citizens and visitors what awaited them if they did not toe the mark.

Zavala, a youth of twenty-two, had an unsavory reputation as a delinquent, but combined that with personal charisma. The townspeople both admired and feared him: He "dishonored young girls and married women," insulted clergymen, made fun of the authorities, and had escaped from prison. He was an expert gambler and swordsman. There are two versions of who started the fatal conflict between Zavala and the Governor, depending on which side the onlooker took. Did the Governor fire unprovoked or did Zavala attack him first? In any case the Swordsman was shot and killed by the Governor as he was trying to seek santuary in the church.

Life is quiet in Cuenca now, as it has been for many years, but the past is ever present in the South American cities I visited, whether it is preconquest or European. Zavala the Swordsman is just a romantic story, but the Frenchmen, during their five years in Cuenca, made a lasting impression. They brought with them a hint of far places, of unfamiliar intellectual pursuits. They stimulated the curiosity of the inhabitants of a city in the wilds, where the exotic culture of Europe was an absolute novelty. Cuenca's citizens, isolated among the forest and snowy mountains, were never really out of the world again.

Two girls, many oranges—Cuenca market

Through an Ingapirca archway

ECUADOR

Darkness at Noon

PRiMERCAPiTVLODLOSiĩ
ARMÁPROPIAS

Heraldic arms of the Inca

The Royal Inca must have been as strange looking to Spaniards as they were to him. His tunic was of finest cumpi weave. He wore ribbons around his ankles and knees, and on his feet were white woolen sandals. His symbol of power was a braid of several colors wrapped around his head, with a red fringe and gold-tipped tassels hanging down. At its highest point the braid held three small black and white feathers of the sacred Curikinga bird. His hair was cut short, also a symbol of his high position. His ears were pierced and distended with huge gold disks the size of oranges. An embroidered coca bag hung by his side. His mien must have been truly regal. He used to say, "The very birds in my realm do not dare to sing against my will."

Cuenca's history predated, of course, the arrival of the Spaniards in the 16th century. It was a chosen retreat of emperors. Huaya Capac, one of the greatest of Inca rulers, was born there, in what was then called Tomebamba, and preferred it to all other cities, saying of it: "A land so serene that none outdoes it in all this realm."

Cieza wrote of Cuenca: "The lodgings of Tomebamba are situated at the joining of two small rivers in a plain having a circumference of over twelve leagues. It is a chilly land, abounding in game such as deer, rabbits, partridges, turtledoves. . . The temple of the sun was of stones put together with the subtlest skill, some of them large, black and rough, and others that seemed of jasper. Some of the Indians claimed that most of the stones used in the construction of these lodgings and the temple of the sun had been brought all the way from Cuzco by order of the Lord-Inca, Huayna Capac."

In the Inca Empire there were many royal dwellings. It was easy to compare them for each ruler left his personal residence decorated and furnished, standing just as he left it, when he went to join the company of mummies. The one at Tomebamba was ranked among the fairest. Inca Huayna Capac, who built it said of it that it was "one of the finest and richest of all Peru, and the buildings the largest and best." The Spaniards concurred, referring to the "sumptuous palaces of Tomebamba."

Cieza tells us: "The fronts of some of the buildings were set with precious stones and emeralds, and, inside, covered with sheets of fine gold. The roofs of thatch were so well laid that, barring a fire, they would last for ages. Inside there were sheafs of golden straw, and on the walls carved figures of the same rich metal, and birds and many other things." One of the palace's treasures was a gold statue of Mama Ocllo, wherein was kept Huayna Capac's sacred placenta.

Huayna Capac was ruler of all Peru, but he preferred Tomebamba to Cuzco, the traditional center of the realm. He had numerous sons of whom Huascar, the legitimate heir, was to rule the Cuzco portions of the empire, while Huayna Capac planned to leave the northern region, with Tomebamba as its capital, to his favorite illegitimate son, Atahuallpa. The realm had never been divided before. This was calling for trouble between the brothers. It led to dissention and civil war, and the killing of thousands of warriors on both sides. If the Inca Empire had not been so divided and weakened the Spaniards could probably not have conquered it.

***

That's getting ahead of the story. The Incas had no advance warning, other than vague prophecies of the end of the world, that strange hostile beings were approaching. The first actual news of Pizarro's landing reached the Emperor at Tomebamba in a weird form, as recorded by Father Cobo: "One day Huayna Capac was taking his ease at his palace in Tomebamba ... when *chasqui* messengers reported that strange people had landed on the beach at Tombes ... white men with beards ... They traveled by sea in great wooden houses ... where they slept at night ... and by day they went ashore ..." So much for the runner's factual account. However, no doubt he had to heighten the effect, to attract the Emperor's full attention and sharpen his belief: "My lord ... the lions and wild animals you have in your palaces there crouched to the ground before them and wagged their tails as if they were tame."

Conqueror's ships

Huayna Capac's son Atahuallpa also received reports with interesting details. The men and animals were an entity; if separated they would die. The animals had silver feet. They were harmless at night. Those long things that spouted thunderbolts could only do so twice. The steel swords of the newcomers were ineffectual; they couldn't hurt anyone. A chief had managed surreptitiously to pour a libation of corn chicha down a gun barrel to solace the thunder box.

***

Chasquis, messenger -runners, aided in administration of the Inca empire

About this time all sorts of dreadful omens were observed. *Chasquis* brought news of mountains which had collapsed. Three large haloes encircled the moon. Lightning struck the Tomebamba palace. A comet with a green tail streamed through the sky, and a sick eagle fell in the palace grounds.

Sorcerers had foretold the arrival of the str*f*angers on their floating islands, and the disasters they would bring. For the sorcerers were specialists. The universe was a big volume full of information, which showed them the future clearly. Knowledge might come through a rainbow, an earthquake, even a line of birds flying across the blue sky. Nothing was meaningless, nothing surprising, although only the few were able to interpret it.

The worst omen of all struck suddenly. Soon after the arrival of the white men, plague spread through the Inca Empire. To us it is evident that the disease was brought by the invaders and passed on to natives who had no immunity to it. It was probably smallpox. The Incas believed it was sent from the great gods to announce the end of the world.

Sorcerers also handled Inca medical problems. There was a list of known cures: hummingbird flesh for epilepsy, a poultice of vicuña meat for eye problems, broth from stewing a young condor for madness. A

Sorcerers

painful area on the skin might be rubbed with a piece of guinea pig to destroy the infection. Everything was allied with incantations, for medicine and magic went hand in hand.

None of this cured the "Running Sickness" which spread rapidly throughout the Empire. No one was safe. Prayers to the great god Inti were not answered. A man could be working his field and his wife, walking behind him to break up the clods, might give a sudden cry and fall to the ground stricken. Children died along with their parents. Nobles were no more immune than commoners, the "worthless people", and the terror spread. In Cuzco kisses were blown to the sacred mountain, snow-capped Ausangate. Terrified people crouched in groups, biting their clothes and tearing the cloth with their teeth, to express fear and horror.

An *itu* was undertaken in Cuzco. For two days everyone fasted and a terrible silence filled Leisure Square. As usual on solemn occasions, dogs and foreigners were expelled from the city. At sunrise on the third day the nobles put on red robes, feather headdresses, shell necklaces. They carried bright green dried birds and white drums.

Officials and commoners filled the great square, everyone silent, mantles over their heads. On the hills above the city a sacrifice was offered. Two fine young children were made drunk with *akha*, then strangled and offered to propitiate the supreme god, Viracocha.

Now the mighty Lords, the Capac Incas, paraded solemnly around Leisure Square beating drums discordantly, and making horrible grimaces, as their women followed behind carrying their slings and spears. One man followed the procession scattering coca leaves. This whole ceremony was carried out eight times between sunset and sunrise.

Such a solemn ritual must surely have placated both Inti and Viracocha. The Incas, reassured, found it time now to eat, drink, and make merry for the danger must be past.

However, almost at once a *chasqui* messenger arrived on the run, bringing word that the great Emperor, Huayna Capac, had been felled by the plague on Quito. Cieza tells us that in that northern capital "so great was the weeping that . . . birds fell stupified from the sky."

Huayna Capac was the last successful absolute monarch among the Incas. He knew how to rule. He is said to have remarked that "to keep the people of these kingdoms well in hand it is a good thing, when they have nothing else to do or busy themselves with, to make them move a mountain from one spot to another." When the Spaniards arrived in the New World the huge Inca empire included two million square kilometers of land with twenty million inhabitants. Yet the Spaniards, less than two hundred strong, subdued the kingdom. The civil war, the running sickness, and native superstititions made it possible.

The strangers might herald the return of the god, Viracocha, who had disappeared long ago into the sea. That would mean the end of the world, perhaps by fire, or perhaps, as it had begun, by flood. Time, which had no meaning as it passed, suddenly assumed one: the end of time, to match the other concept of time's beginning.

The empire now split into two parts, with Huascar taking over at Cuzco as Magnificent and Unique Inca, and marrying his sister, Golden Ecstatic Joy. He was the first emperor to claim actual divinity, with the title *Inti Illapa*, God and Thunder.

Atahuallpa on his throne

Huayna Capac's mummy was brought from Quito to Cuzco but Atahuallpa, his favorite son, remained in the north. In due course word was brought from Tomebamba by a speical *chasqui*, a top runner identified by a white feather headdress. For his audience the *chasqui* approached Huascar with a burden on his back, placed there at the last guard post outside the city. This showed his submission to supreme power.. Removing his sandals, he walked backwards into the royal presence. He used a formal greeting, "Hail, unique Inca!" and, when he turned to deliver his message he saw the Inca's face only vaguely, through a thin cloth held in front of him by a couple of lovely girls. Atahuallpa, he said, had taken over all the northern territory.

***

Incidents of insult and rebellion increased between the two brothers until the war was open, although it was never declared. There were skirmishes, plots, counterplots and confrontations. At the end of it all Atahuallpa had been captured by the invaders, Huascar had been killed. It was indeed the *pachatikray*, the "end of the world." Soon Spaniards arrived in Cuzco to superintend the prying off of sheets of gold from walls, to collect silver and objects, enlisting special bearers to take it all to Cajamarca as part of the ranson for Atahuallpa's life.

***

In the war between the brothers about 200,000 Indians were killed. The enormous kingdom was now ripe for takeover by a handful of adventurers. Francisco Pizarro felt that he had every right to be there. Hadn't the King of Spain bestowed this land on him. He entered South America with a commission empowering him to proceed to Peru. His coat of arms showed a llama, and bore the title, "Governor and Captain General of Peru."

Atahuallpa was enjoying the baths at Cajamarca when the Spaniards left the coast to take over their assignment as the new rulers of Peru. He had with him some 30,000 retainers, and there was surely no doubt in his mind that *he* was the ruler of Peru. He had his own coat of arms, more elaborate than Pizarro's. It included a falcon between two trees, a couple of snakes, and a puma reclining under a rainbow.

During their journey from the coast to Cajamarca the Spaniards were not attacked, though they were watched carefully. On November 15, 1532, they entered the central square of

Atahuallpa carried from the baths

Cajamarca. It was deserted. Atahuallpa, with his hordes of followers, had camped at a spring outside the city. Pizzaro sent Hernando de Soto with a band of cavalry to invite the Inca to visit him, at which time he planned to capture the Emperor. Thinking his first emissaries too few, he sent another force to overtake them. To have been one of those sent to treat with the Inca was an honor never forgotten. Atahuallpa first made the Spaniards wait for an interview, then agreed to visit the next day. He sent Pizarro a pair of painted shoes and some gold bracelets so the Inca could recognize him.

To the Incas the Spaniards looked like corpses when they arrived in the cold mountains, wrapped like mummies, with woolen scarves over their faces, caps like little red pots sitting on their heads so that only their fierce eyed looked out. The horses were even stranger than the men. They might be human too — after all they ate maize — and some of the Indians, when they sent gifts to Piazrro, offered sacred virgins to the horses as well as to the men.

The Royal Inca must have been as strange looking to Spaniards as they were to him. His tunic was of finest *cumpi* weave. He wore ribbons around his ankles and knees, and on his feet were white woolen sandals. His symbol of power was a braid of several colors wrapped around his head, with a red fringe and gold-tipped tassels hanging down. At its highest point the braid held three small black and white feathers of the sacred Curikinga bird. His hair was cut short, also a symbol of his high position. His ears were pierced and distended with huge gold disks the size of oranges. An embroidered coca bag hung by his side. His mien must have been truly regal. He used to say, "The very birds in my realm do not dare to sing against my will." Surely not strange man-beasts, or whatever they were, would have the courage to confront him and his thousands of retainers.

The next day negotiations went on. First, the Inca would come unarmed; on second thought he would come armed. By late afternoon he had approached to within a few hundred yards of the Spaniards. He advanced toward the square, riding on a solid gold litter (it weighed a hundred pounds the chroniclers noted). It was carried by sixteen bearers. Hundreds of nobles in checked livery accompanied the ruler to sweep straw and pebbles out of the way. They were chanting a song, loudly and in unison. They were fully armed with maces and slings. One witness tells us that many of the Spaniards were so terrified that "they could not hold their water."

However, the plan for capture had been carefully made. The friar, Vicente de Valverde, was to approach the Inca making a gesture of peace. Then the invaders would suddenly launch a noisy attack, with the music of fifes and drums, punctuated by a roar of gunshots.

It went as planned, far easier than expected. Pizarro stepped forward.

"St. James and at them!"

The Spaniards charged. The Inca fell from his litter, abandoned by his retinue. There was a total rout, with hundreds, perhaps thousands, of Indians killed as they fled the terrifying guns and horses.

The supreme ruler, the great Inca, Atahuallpa, in the Spaniards' hands, changed his golden litter for a seat on the mud floor of a hut.

**

Atahuallpa's fate was undecided for some weeks, during which time he was chained and guarded, sitting sadly on the floor of his prison. The Spaniards were busy receiving llama troops bearing loot. It was said that Atahuallpa, a comparatively young man in his thirties, even though reduced in this humiliating way from his royal state, was "always carefully groomed and extremely clean ... He never spat on the ground but always in the hand of a woman, out of dignity."

Atahuallpa in prison

He must have been a sympathetic human being, not just an impassive god figure. Tradition has it that he made some friends among the Spaniards. He became a very good chess player, a game which he called by the Indian word *taptana* or "suprise attack."

The terms for Atahuallpa's release, as agreed to by Pizarro, were that treasure should be delivered, a ransom of gold, silver and jewels, in quantity to fill a room 20 x 17 feet to a height of 9 feet. Word was sent out and Indians with llamas and loads of precious metal trudged from hundreds of miles away to rescue their sacred ruler.

An unbelievable mass of treasure was brought to Cajamarca, the room was filled, but Atahuallpa was not immediately released. There was disagreement among the Spaniards. They could keep him in prison, they could make him a puppet ruler, they could send him as a prisoner to Spain. The decision was made, however, to execute him, perhaps for safety's sake to avert future uprisings. A vote was taken and 50 of the 300 Spaniards were against this treacherous plan, but the motion was carried. A mock trial was held with all sorts of trumped-up charges and the Inca was condemned to death.

First, however, he should be converted to Christianity. Atahuallpa was of course illiterate (as was Francisco Pizarrro for that matter), and one of the things the Indians first noted about the strange invaders was their preoccupation with books and papers. It was rumored that they talked with these day and night.

When Atahuallpa was handed a bible and urged to become Christian he said, "Let that book speak to me."

When it was handed to him he turned the pages, keeping an eye on it, and listening. Finally, disenchanted, he said, "Why doesn't the book speak to me?" and threw it on the ground.

As an unbeliever the Inca was sentenced to be burned alive. At the last minute, however, when he professed Christianity and received baptism the sentence was changed to death by strangling.

It should be noted that his reason for conversion was not that he heard the book speak, or that the friars convinced him. He believed that if his body was consumed and destroyed by fire he could not live on as a mummy through the ages, dead but not dead, in a timeless existence fulfilling his natural destiny.

In executing Atahuallpa, Francisco Pizarro had made a false move. King Charles of Spain was furious that anyone should presume to kill a king, even in a distant heathen land. Surely it made a dangerous precedent.

On the day of the Inca's death, it is said a band of Indians were approaching Cajamarca with 7,000 llamas loaded with gold for the ranson. On hearing the dreadful news they hurled the treasure into a thermal pond of steaming water nearby. Word of Atahuallpa's death spread quickly through the kingdom and consignments of ransom were hidden in caves, buried in the ground, tossed into Lake Titicaca. No wonder people have been seeking treasure for centuries in Inca territory. No one knows how much of the unbelievable ransom has been discovered and secretly removed over the intervening centuries. The sort of publicity engendered by raising sunken ships would not be necessary here — just some strong carrying sacks and a horde of obedient llamas.

Atahuallpa's execution

On the volcano Cotopaxi, near Quito, there is a memorial to Inca times, a rock resembling an Indian face turned upward toward the sun. The legend is that on the day Atahuallpa was strangled the rock fell away from the cliff, leaving the likeness of the Emperor as a reminder forever.

The death of Atahuallpa is still remembered in folklore. It has been dramatized in Quechua elegies and songs of sorrow passed down through generations.

> *The cruel whites*
> *Who were seeking gold*
> *Invaded us like a plague.*
> *After capturing our Father Inca,*
> *After gaining his trust,*
> *They gave him death.*
> *With the savagery of the puma,*
> *With the cunning of the fox, —*
> *As if he were a llama*
> *They slaughtered him.*

These Quechua laments are often general, expressing simply a state of mind, a pervasive melancholy, an extension of the Indian woman's cry, when she heard of the Inca's death" "Darkness fell at noon."

> *I am night without an end,*
> *I am loneliness without relief,*
> *I am the very soul of anguish,*
> *I am fleeing from my own thoughts.*

***

On my last day in Cuenca I walked along the Tomebamba River. Washerwomen were spreading clothes on the rocks to dry, university students sauntered along the banks gossiping about their own affairs, and water rippled briskly under the bridge, close to the enormous boulders which are the only remains of Huayna Capac's sumptuous palace. Looking up at the sky with its fluffy clouds I noticed the afternoon jet from Guayaquil swooping down for a landing.

bird scaring method

A bird perched on the bushes near where I stood. It was followed by another and another. I thought of the Curikinga, the sacred Inca bird. Atahuallpa, as supreme ruler, wore feathers of this bird in his royal headdress. It was native to the Tomebamba area, and so numerous that, even a few years ago, it was an annoyance to local farmers, following their plows to feed on earthworms, and even attacking the men. The meat of these birds was not good, but a drink of their blood was said to give courage. The flocks of Curikingas have now been decimated by the use of pesticides and, my Cuenca guidebook tells me, they are rarely seen.

It was time to go back to the Crespo Hotel and get my bags, for I was leaving on that plane to Quito. Those birds I saw were probably ordinary mountain doves. Nowadays sacred birds are scarce.

A town church and its reflection—Ecuador

Church at Pisac

EPILOGUE

The conqueror and the conquered.

I considered what I had to show for this trip. I can't claim any thrilling South American adventures.

I enjoyed whatever it is that travel gives me: refreshment, exhilaration, the feeling of having ventured forth for a while from my usual little segment of the world.

Threshold T he Lima airport is a great place to sit and think. My plane to Mexico City was scheduled to depart, like Cinderella's coach, at midnight precisely. I was there at ten-thirty, ready to clear my possessions and myself for the trip.

Nothing doing. "You're too early," the desk clerk said.

"When should I check in?"

"Don't worry. We'll call the flight."

I therefore sat and thought, naturally, of my excursion just ending and my future plans. I did hope to make still another journey to South America — next time Colombia? Argentina? It would be a year, at least, before I could come this way again.

Meanwhile I thought about the differences between the area I had just visited and Mexico, where I have lived for more than a decade.

Their history was in many ways parallel. Francisco Pizarro was harsher in his conquest of Peru than Cortes had been in Mexico, although the results were much the same: death and destruction for the Indian inhabitants, a gradual change to Spanish-style civilization, a slow merging of races.

The conquests took place at almost the same time. In each country a handful of Spaniards entered, fortuitously, at a time when there was internal disruption in a multi-tribal empire. They were able to conquer by wile, and by the force of their strangeness and possible relationship to divinities. Cortes might well be the Plumed Serpent, Pizarro the great god Viracocha returned from the sea.

It is interesting that now, 450 years later, the Mexicans have obliterated all memories of Cortes from their cities. You will find no street or plaza named for him, no monument to his memory. Children are often named Montezuma or Cuauhtemoc; they are not named Cortes. In Lima, however, Pizarro's mummified body lies in state in a glass coffin in the cathedral, and his statue presides over one of the main squares. Perhaps the reason for this lies in the way the two countries have developed. In Mexico, while there are still many Indians in outlying areas, the mass of the population is *mestizo*, "mixed."

In the Andes cities, on the other hand, Indians remain a race apart, millions of them still speaking Quechua instead of Spanish. The Europeanized population lives a cosmopolitan life in the cities, where Spain does not seem as far away as the nearby indigenous villages. Perhaps I am wrong about this, but, living as a foreigner in one country and visiting as a foreigner in another, that was how it struck me.

I considered what I had to show for this trip. I can't claim any thrilling South American adventures. I didn't have my toes nibbled by pirhanas or frostbitten on the frigid slopes of Cotopaxi. No anacondas dropped on me from trees. No messages reached me from another world.

Almagro and Pizarro

I enjoyed whatever it is that travel gives me: refreshment, exhilaration, the feeling of having ventured forth for a while from my usual little segment of the world.

My thoughts were interrupted by a tap on the shoulder. Ah - Señora Mendez and her daughter, whom I last saw in Arequipa when Juan and I met them at the airport.

"We are going to Iquitos," she told me. "I want Blanca to see the Amazon."

Blanca yawned. She didn't look carried away with the idea of the Amazon. She was exchanging glances with a young German on the next bench.

We went into the restaurant for coffee together, since Señora Mendez' flight was delayed. We ended by having an ice cream for Blanca and more coffee for the Señora and me, meanwhile checking her flight from time to time. Jack, an American I had met in Machu Picchu now joined us. We had more coffee. He was trying to fly to Miami but the airlines had no record of his reservation although his ticket read "reconfirmed."

"I just now saw you," he told me sadly. "I've been waiting around here for half the day. We could have taken a cab together and gone downtown."

I agreed. He shook his head. "On second thought, no we couldn't. I'm supposed to check in with the airline every half hour in case there's a cancellation.

The Señora and Blanca left us. They had changed to the other airline which promised to take off for the Amazon in a jiffy. Blanca yawned again as they said goodbye and hurried off to the boarding gate. Jack went to check his Miami reservation. I looked at my watch. Eleven-thirty already, and they hadn't called my flight. I went to the ticket counter.

"Delayed. We'll announce it."

I sat quietly, too revved up with coffee to read a book.

It was twelve-thirty. The magic hour of midnight had passed. Again there was a tap on my shoulder. Señora Mendez and Blanca were back again. Now it was one-thirty.

"The flight didn't go to Iquitos?"

The Señora laughed. "Oh yes, we flew there but we couldn't land. Too much mud on the field. We'll have to go into the city and look for a room." We parted again, this time finally.

I inquired at the airline desk. "When will you announce the flight to Mexico?"

"We didn't announce it; they are already boarding."

I hurried to present papers, check my baggage. Then I went into the usual airport holding room where the other passengers had already gathered. We watched through the window while our baggage was loaded. I don't usually check my things, but at the very end of a trip it's different. I can't resist alpaca sweaters, woven wall hangings, the usual loot which brings back pleasant memories. I saw my suitcase being hurled mercilessly into the hold. Then the boarding ramp was wheeled out and grabbed our plane in its teeth.

So now I was returning to Mexico, regretfully leaving Peru. But not so soon there! As Victor pointed out to me in the La Paz airport, you aren't leaving until you are actually airborne. Suddenly a voice spoke from a microphone.

"All passengers on this flight will now return to the city. We are not boarding until noon. (It was now two a.m.) Be back here at ten. Please note also that you must enter Peru again since you have relinquished your visas and are no longer in the country."

A Latin American businessman rushed furiously at the girl, threatening her. "This is not to be tolerated! You will take us to Mexico now!"

The girl smiled a thoughtful, perfidious smile. "Not our fault. We cannot land in Mexico. The whole country is on stike, the airport there is closed. You must not blame this on Peru."

The man was nt longer threatening, only frustrated. He clumped back to his seat. The girl winked and grinned behind his back.

All sixty passengers did indeed enter the country again. When it came my turn to enter Peru the immigration officer wrote statistics from my passport onto his form, stamped the paper, called for my signature, laid aside the original and passed me the copy which I would give back at exit in the morning. He had forgotten the carbon paper.

"There's nothing on this visa." I waved it at him with wild foreign agitation. "Look! This copy says nothing."

The immigration man adjusted his glasses and frowned at the interruption. "At this time of the night, Señorita, what does it matter?" He blew his nose and got to the next passenger.

In the morning I approached the check-in desk with apprehension. Yes. Yes, our plane was actually leaving ... We would be reunited with our baggage which held everything incommunicado on board during the night ... We were going to fly ... We were going to Mexico City from which lately came that weird untrue rumor that the airport was closed ... We were about to enter the friendly embrace of a plane called, happily, "The Inca."

My relief was interrupted as I passed through the line at immigration.

"What is this? A blank sheet of paper!" The officer's bark brought me back to modern problems, far from the Incas. He glared. Yes, of course I was at fault, guilty of everything, whatever it was. Shortly there might be a body search for cocaine.

"I entered Peru last night very late," I stammered. "It was two o'clock in the morning. No carbon paper in my visa. The officer said that, at that hour, Señor, it didn't matter.

The immigration man tried on his furious expression, laid it aside and smiled. He waved me along to the boarding gate. "It's half past ten in the morning now, Señorita."

He tossed my blank visa into a wastebasket. He smiled warmly. "We are friendly people in Peru, Señorita. It doesn't matter at this time of day either. We will just forget you were ever here."

Pisac girls

Abecia, Valentin. La Dramatica Historica del Mar Boliviano. La Paz, Bolivia: Liberia Editorial "Juventud", 1986.

_____. Historia de Chuquisaca. Sucre, Bolivia: Editorial Charcas, 1939.

Adorno, Rolena. Guaman Poma, Writing and Resistance in Colonial Peru. Austin, Texas: University of Texas Press, 1986.

Aeroperu. Report on Peru. Cuzco, Peru: Envolturas Comerciales S.A., 1977.

Baudin, Louis. Daily Life in Peru Under The Incas. New York: Macmillan, 1962.

Bennet, Wendell C. and Bird, Junius B. Andrean Cultural History. New York: Natural History Press, 1964.

Boero Rojo, Hugo. Bolivia Magica. La Paz, Bolivia: Editorial "Los Amigos del Libor", 1978.

Bowen, David. The Land and People of Peru. Philadelphia and New York: Lippincott, 1963.

Brand, Lieut. Charles, RN. Journal of a Voyage to Peru in the Winter of 1827. London: 1828.

Brooks, John, editor. The 1986 South American Handbook. Bath, England: 1985.

Brundage, Burr Cartwright. Empire of the Inca. Norman, Okla.: University of Oklahoma, 1963.

_____. Lords of Cuzco. Norman, Okla.: University of Oklahoma, 1967.

Carletti, Francesco. My Voyage Around the World 1594-96. New York: Pantheon, 1964.

Cieza de Leon. The Incas. Edited by Victor Wolfgang von Hagen. Norman, Okla.: University of Oklahoma, 1959.

Clark, E. B. Twelve Months in Peru. London: Unwin, 1891.

Cuenca. Tourist Guide of Azuay and Canar. Cuenca, Ecuador: 1978.

de Carvalho-Neto, Paulo. Folklore Poetico. Quito, Ecuador: Editorial Universitaria and S. Houser, 1966.

Eichler, Arturo. Ecuador, A Land, A People, A Culture. Quito, Ecuador: Libri Mundi, 1982.

Frazier, Charles, with Donal Secreast. Adventuring in the Andes. San Francisco Sierra Club Books, 1985.

Fresco, Antonio. La Archeologia de Ingapirca (Ecuador). Cuena, Ecuador: Comision del Castillo de Ingapirca, 1984.

Furneaux, Robin. The Amazon. New York: Putnam, 1970.

Garcilaso de la Vega. The Incas. The Royal Commentaries of the Inca Garcilaso de la Vega 1539–1616. New York: The Orion Press, 1961.

Gheerbrant, Edmond J. The Inca Garcilaso. New York: Orion, 1961.

Goodman, Edmond J. The Explorers of South America. New York: Macmillan, 1972.

Guidoni, Enrico and Roberto Magni, Monuments of Civilization, The Andes. New York: Grosset & Dunlap, 1977.

Guzman, Augusto, Beve Historia de Bolivia. La Paz, Bolivia: Enciclopedia Boliviana Editorial "Los Amigos del Libro," 1969.

Hamlyn, Paul, South American Mythology. Fletham, Middlesex, England: Hamlyn House, 1969.

Hill, S. S. Travels in Peru and Mexico. London: Layman & Roberts, 1860.

Huaman Poma, Felipe. Letter to a King. New York: Dutton, 1978.

Ibarra Grasso, Dick. La Verdaera Historia de los Incas. La Paz, Bolivia: Editorial "Los Amigos del Libro", 1978.

Jagendorf, M.A. and Boggs, R. S., The King of the Mountain. New York: Vanguard, 1960.

Krickeberg, Walter, Mitos y Leyendas de los Aztecas, Incas, Mayas, y Muiscas. Mexico: Fonda de Cultura Economica, 1971.

Lara, Jesuw. La Poesia Quechua. Mexico: Fonda de Cultura Economica, 1971.

Leonard, Irving A., editor. Colonial Travelers in Latin America. New York: Knopf, 1972.

Lockhard, James. The Men of Cajamarca. Austin, Texas: Univesity of Texas, 1972.

Machicago, Humberto Vazquez, Jose de Mesa y Teresa Gisbert. Manual de Historia de Bolivia. La Paz, Bolivia: Gisbert y Cia., 1983.

Mason, J. Alden, The Ancient Civilization of Peru. Middlesex, England, 1961.

Matthiessen, Peter. The Cloud Forest. New York: Viking, 1961.

McIntyre, Loren. The Incredible Incas. Washington, D.C. National Geographic Society, 1975.

Meisch, Lynn. A Traveler's Guide to El Dorado and the Inca Empire. New York: Viking–Penguin, 1984.

Paredes-Candia, Antonio. Adivinanzas Bolivianas. La Paz, Bolivia: Ediciones Isla, 1977.

_____. Antonlogia de Tradiciones y Leyendas Bolivianas. La Paz, Boliva: Editorial "Los Amigos del Libro," 1974.

_____. Fiestas Popular de Bolivia. Vol. I and II. La Paz, Bolivia: Ediciones Isla y Librereia-Editorial Popular, 1976.

Pierce, Frank. Amadis de Gaula. Boston: C.K. Hall, 1976.

Quesda, Vincente G., Cronicas Potosinas, Vol. II. Potosi, Bolivia: Sociedad Georgrafica y de Historia Positi., 1951.

Ramirez del Ciguia, Lic. Noticias Politicas de Indians y Relacion Descriptiva, de la Ciudad de la Plata. Sucre, Bolivia: Don Thomas Remays de Vargas, 1978.

Salomon, Frank. Native Lords of Quito in the Age of the Incas. New York: Cambridge University Press, 1986.

Shichor, Michael. Michael's Guide to South America, vol. 2. England: Inbal, Travel Information LTD, 1985.

Sitwell, Sacheverell. Golden Wall and Mirador. London: Weidenfeld & Nicolson, 1961.

Vidal, Humberto. Vision del Cuzao. Cuzco, Peru: Universidad del Cuzco, 1958.

Ullopa, Joyrge Juan & Antonia de la Conadmine, 1735-
   A Voyage to South America 1748. New York: Knopf, 1964.

Von Hagen, Victor Wolfgang. The Ancient Sun Kingdom of the
   America. New York: World, 1961.

_____ . The Golden Man. London:
   Saxon House, 1974.

_____ . South America Callec Them.
   New York: Knopf, 1945.

Whymper, Edward. Travels Amongst The Great Andea of the Equator.
   Salt Lake City: Peregine Smith books, 1987.

Zarate, Augustin de, A History of the Discovery and Conquest of Peru.
   London: Penguin, 1933.

Zeballas Barrios, Carlos O. Arequipa Con Todo Su Valor.
   Arequipa, Peru: Ediciones Turisticas, 1980.

BOLIVIA, 76-101, 45-73
historical notes & annotations, 88-89, 97-77, 47-52, 67, 69-71

La Paz, 57-65
Chacaltaya, 64
Potosí, 82-88, 93-94
historical notes & annotations, 82-86, 91-93, 94-96
Puno, 53-55
Sucre, 76-80
historical notes & annotations, 80-81
Taquile, 57
Tihuanaku, 67, 69-71

ECUADOR, 126-131, 134-145, 148-153, 156-167
historical notes & annotations, 156-167

Cuenca, 134-139, 143-145, 148, 166
historical notes & annotations, 138, 148-153, 156
Ingapirca, 141
panama hats, 143-144
Otavalo, 122
Quito, 116-120, 123, 126
historical notes & annotations, 126-131
Santo Domingo de los Colorados, 122-123

PERU, 6-43, 104-113
historical notes & annotations, 6

Arequipa, 104-111
historical notes & annotations, 112
Canyon de Colca, 108
Cuzco, 13-18, 21, 34-36, 41-42
Cuzco Valley, 13
historical notes & annotations, 20-21, 23, 38-41
Machu Picchu, 29-34
historical notes & annotations, 32, 33
Sacred Inca Valley, 24-25

llamas, 28-29, 67, 108-110
maps,